I dedicate this book to:

My business partner, Rob, without whom this book
wouldn't have been possible. His direction and
unwavering support in creating the structure and content
to launch *Uncommon Sense* have been invaluable. I owe
him a great debt.
Gemma, my fiancée, for providing sound advice,
inspiration, unconditional love and space to grow.
My parents – my mother, Catherine, and my stepfather
of almost two decades, William – thank you both for
providing the fertile ground that helped me develop and
for your continuous support.
And my late father, Stuart, who provided me with
a first-class education and introduced me to the
'uncommon sense' concept.

Uncommon Sense

The popular misconceptions of business, investing and finance, and how to profit by going against the tide

MARK HOMER

First published in Great Britain in 2017 by John Murray Learning.
An Hachette UK company.
Copyright © Mark Homer 2017
The right of Mark Homer to be identified as the Author of the Work has been asserted by
him in accordance with the Copyright, Designs and Patents Act 1988.
Database right: Hodder & Stoughton (makers)
British Library Cataloguing in Publication Data: a catalogue record for this title is available
from the British Library.
Library of Congress Catalog Card Number: on file.
Trade paperback ISBN 978 1 473 65768 7
Paperback ISBN 978 1 473 65769 4
eBook ISBN 978 1 473 65770 0
1

Typeset by Cenveo Publisher Services.
Printed and bound in Great Britain by CPI Group (UK) Ltd, Croydon, CR0 4YY.
John Murray Learning policy is to use papers that are natural, renewable and recyclable
products and made from wood grown in sustainable forests. The logging and manufacturing
processes are expected to conform to the environmental regulations of the country of origin.

Carmelite House
50 Victoria Embankment
London EC4Y 0DZ
www.hodder.co.uk

Contents

Part 3: Strategies and tactics

Part 4: Additional resources

Introduction

A lemming is a 'small, short-tailed, thickset rodent related to the voles, found in the Arctic tundra'. It is also a 'person who unthinkingly joins a mass movement, especially a headlong rush to destruction'. Many investors and business owners are lemmings. They blindly follow what the media, their friends and perceived investment experts advise, most usually into investments that have performed very well in the previous few years, and so are presumed to be good for the future, and for their money.

In the early stages, it can feel both safe and exciting to invest like a lemming, but before you know it you are following the masses off a cliff towards financial suicide. The keyword in the above definition is 'blindly': without diligence, knowledge, research or experience. Lemmings make blind decisions under the assumption that, if everyone else is doing it, it must be right. And if it goes wrong, there is safety in numbers again. You don't look too stupid and you can easily point the finger of blame at someone else.

This, of course, is not new or revelatory. The 'herd mentality' has been with us through humanity for as long as we were big enough as a species to be part of a herd or tribe. The feeling of safety in numbers is a reality. In modern life, this herd mentality has translated into connectivity, networks like the Internet, mainstream mass media, and social networks. Opinions are grouped rather than individual, and therefore mass opinion has weight and can shift very quickly, with huge momentum. This mass opinion does not always translate well into business, finance and investing because it is often wrong. If mass opinion was right, a 'contrarian' wouldn't exist and everyone would be 'doing it'. It is often the case that the loudest voices are the ones that the masses listen to and are blindly influenced by. Yet, being loud doesn't increase the value or validity of their opinion. In fact, often by the very nature of being the loudest, those opinions are typically the furthest from reality.

Instead of independently seeking out high-quality and well-researched information, herding sees people simply observing the actions of others as a guide to sensible behaviour. In business, finance, and investing, a swarm of individuals with a lemming-like blind faith in assets and market trends can lead to boom-and-bust cycles, mispricing of assets, as well as poor business and investment decisions by the individual.

I don't want to digress too much, but understanding why we have this mentality can surely help us embrace the benefits and drawbacks, understand the thought processes and instincts that serve us for business, finance and investing, and those we need to master. After all, if lemming-like herding is so dangerous in modern business and investing, why did it evolve in the first place and what purpose does it still serve?

According to an article in *Psychology Today*, herding actually evolved to benefit individuals, not groups or societies:

> We're used to thinking of social groups as fundamentally cooperative entities, but with some kinds of groups, nothing could be further from the truth. In fact, the best-known biological theory of herding, William Hamilton's 'selfish herd' idea, proposes that herds are the result of individuals trying to ensure that other members of their species, rather than themselves, will get eaten by predators.

> Dr Michael E. Price, *Psychology Today*

Price's argument suggests that herding is very much a selfish act to preserve self-interest. If this argument is to be believed, there is some (un)common sense in it – particularly in that it serves the interest of the individual to follow the herd for survival and, in more modern times, social acceptance. This is ironic because, in most areas of business, finance and investing, it does the opposite, and yet the protagonist is blind to it, or at least the emotions of acceptance and rejection are too strong. Our primal instincts haven't evolved as fast as modern society. They do not reflect the need to survive and thrive in business and investing, but still serve to protect us on a basic survival level.

Price says that another likely reason for herding is that groups can more easily benefit from knowledge that other group members have gained about, for example, the location of resources. 'Herding can thus improve individual foraging success ... herding is the by-product of individuals pursuing their own self-interest.'

This has certainly carried forward and can benefit people in modern society. If you want to see a film, watch the one with the best reviews and recommendations. If you want to be sure of a seller on eBay, look through their feedback. If you want to hire someone, talk to their previous employers and peers. In this way you will significantly reduce the risk of a failure or bad decision, with minimal time input or wastage. People consciously and unconsciously apply the same logic to their financial affairs and decisions. They look to save time and gain experience from society, a concept that is commonly known as 'social proof'. To a certain degree, there is logic and common sense in observing the masses, but in business, finance and investing, this is counterproductive because your money is at stake. When your money is at stake, the whole game changes and other variables come into play. Some of these variables are:

- How mass movement into an asset affects (pushes up) the price
- The combined knowledge and experience of the masses not being deep, specific or niched enough
- The blind leading the blind
- Modern business and finance being more complicated than the basic survival instinct
- Social pressure and fear of rejection or judgement by being a 'contrarian'.

Mass speculators often have limited information and experience when it comes to investing in assets and markets. They can perceive that others have better information, are more experienced and/or can save them, so they base their decisions on the actions and social proof of others. This may be fine for a film review where the risk of loss is low or mitigated to a wasted hour or two, but with the high risks associated with business and investing this is not a transferable approach. With the mass of information, marketing and advertising thrown at us everywhere we go, online and offline, our brain has adapted to save time by generalizing information or looking for short cuts. If it didn't, it would explode out of our ears from information overload.

In searching for this leverage of others' experience to save time and follow 'social proof', merged with herding and 'selfish herding', the masses often base their business and investing decisions on:

- what they perceive most people are doing
- time saving as a higher priority than finding the best investment
- the fear of looking socially inadequate and how others perceive them
- feeling good now.

We have already covered the first two on this list.

The third reason, the fear of others' perception, is often a big block to sustainable success in business and investing. If an individual makes decisions based on not looking the fool rather than what is most likely to yield the best return, then perhaps that person is a lemming. For example, if you lose a bet that everyone knew about and no one else made because they all thought it was a hopeless long shot, at best you'll look less competent than everyone else. But if you lose a bet that everyone else made too, because they all thought it was a sure thing, you won't seem any less competent than the others. This strong emotional need to be accepted by others (or not rejected) damages most people's wealth. One has to embrace and master this fear to succeed and sustain wealth for the long run. One has to risk alienation and ridicule in the short term. Can you? Are you prepared to try? If so, read on.

The fourth reason, the need for instant gratification, is a very dangerous risk to your profits. Emotions are strong and addictive because they serve to overpower logic and reason. The addictive chemicals produced by the brain ensure that we act on our emotions and don't override them in certain situations. For example, we frequently allow our emotions to guide our need to self-preserve, procreate, sleep, experience happiness and so on. But in business and investing, many of these emotions negate and overpower smart, well-researched decisions. Just as we can get addicted to sugar, we can also get addicted to a happy feeling, acceptance from others and self-importance. This affects our finances when we allow our emotions about how others perceive our decisions, being accepted and liked, and feeling good about 'spending' money to drive our investing decisions. People frequently fail to succeed as a direct result of letting their emotions drive their decisions instead of facts, research, risk mitigation and value.

A simple example, and one I see on a daily basis, is how people make property investment decisions based on how a property looks, whether they would choose to live in it, that it is new, what other people would say about its appearance, its location, the allure of the colourful brochure, and the perceived status of having a holiday home-cum-investment. This is almost always the wrong way of investing in property. The value is most often in properties that aren't in use, are cosmetically dilapidated, not in the best areas so there is room for growth, have issues that need fixing, and would definitely not double up as a home in which to raise your family. In the early days of my property investing, I was buying some of the ugliest family homes you could wish to see. I learned that the worse they were (cosmetically, not structurally), the more money they made. You certainly wouldn't be showing these off in a glossy photo album to your friends at a private members club.

In summary, Dr Price states that herding, which may seem wise as an individual strategy, can become dangerous at a systemic level when combined with too much optimism and lack of information – and can lead to spectacular market crashes. Speculators often think that others have better information than they do, so they base their decisions on the actions of others. Bubbles in market systems are probably caused less by individuals taking risks and more by people choosing what feels like a safe strategy: following the herd.

In the modern world, where information is a commodity and time our most valuable and scarce resource, I will not waste yours with waffle or hyperbole. You don't need another 18 hours on audio or a 500-page book that you have to wade through to pick out a few gems. In this book, I will investigate and explain how much time you should spend and invest in research, analysis and educating yourself in an asset class, versus how much time you could and should save, leverage or outsource. I will also identify key areas and strategies for saving time where wastage is rife. This will allow you to strategically reinvest those hours into your business models and asset classes for maximum return.

Uncommon Sense will be concise and to the point. It will be candid and sometimes seem to be focusing on mistakes and the negative aspects of business, finance and investing. This is not a personal development happy-clappy-type book; the reality is that we have to deal with challenges and disruptions every day, and to avoid them or fluff around them is a disservice to the smart investor and to you as a reader who wants the reality. This book presents the facts and not the fluff, and provides informed, unbiased information on how to make smart decisions. Overall, I am very positive about business, finance and investing, enjoying them as both a passion and a profession. I hope that shows through, but only you can be the judge of that. These are exciting times. There have never been more opportunities to cash in and leverage new platforms and technologies, but we must keep our feet firmly on the ground, preserve our capital and resources, and learn the best ways to profit by going against the tide.

About Mark Homer

This is awkward for me. I feel uncomfortable shouting about successes, so I have asked Rob Moore, my business partner, to write this section. I understand that you need to know enough about me for me to be credible as the author of Uncommon Sense *and the information I am sharing to be believed. So I will leave this section to him.*

Mark started in business and investing in his early teenage years on the side at school. Mark would buy and sell cars at a profit and ran businesses during the early stages of the Internet. Inspired by his father, partly in what to do and partly in what not to do, Mark saved, invested and lived frugally (living with his mum until age 27) until he had multiple deposit pots to start property investing in 2003. He was in his early twenties when he began to acquire those first properties. Mark shares much of the upbringing that formed his business and investing focus in his popular book *Low Cost High Life: live an affordable life of luxury*. Mark likes to get value out of every penny spent or invested, to the point where he can seem eccentric and extreme. He would credit his father with that trait.

Since 2003, Mark has masterminded the purchase of around 650 properties and then co-founded Progressive Property to manage many of them. He is also the co-owner of an eight-figure training business in property, business and personal development. He is a systems and analysis 'geek' (because he'd hate being called an expert) and thrives on the details and research of business, finance and investing. He has regularly commentated in major publications including the *Telegraph*, the *Wall Street Journal* and *International Business Times*, has appeared on BBC radio and ITV's *Daybreak*, as well as co-authoring the UK's best-selling property book, *Property Investing Secrets*. Mark is a Guinness world record holder for public speaking on business, property and finance.

Since 2003, when he started investing in property, and then again in 2005, when he quit the corporate rat race to become a business owner, Mark has become a (reclusive) multimillionaire. He believes in preserving capital, investing for the long term and not jumping between models and fads so frequently that you can't gain momentum in the classes you are in. He stresses that you should never spend more than you earn, you should invest disposable capital, and you should use the income streams from assets only, never capital, to pay for liabilities and consumer purchases.

Abbreviations used in this book

DR	direct response
FOMO	'fear of missing out'
FT	*Financial Times*
GP	gross product
HMO	house in multiple occupation
IFA	Independent Financial Advisor
IGT	income-generating tasks
IP	intellectual property
JV	joint venture
KPI	key performance indicator
KRA	key result area
LCV	lifetime client value
MAC	maximum acquisition cost
MLM	multi-level marketing
MVP	minimum viable product *or* most valuable player
NM	non-monetary
NP	net profit
PHR	per head revenue
PPC	pay per click
VVMC	values, vision, mission and culture

Part 1: The concept

In this part of the book, I will discuss overriding and enduring philosophies, misconceptions and realities in business, finance and investing. My aim is to present concepts that will stand the test of time and be as relevant 20 years from now as they are today. I will dig into schemes and scams to protect your capital, and detail mistakes, lessons and successes in business, finance and investing, citing precedents, competitors and personal experiences to give you a balanced view.

I

The uncommon sense philosophy

If I were to create a philosophy for uncommon sense business, finance and investing, and how to profit by going against the tide, it would be to be sceptical of mass media information and the weight of common opinion and action. While you should have half an eye on mainstream views and news, you must investigate and research for yourself by looking for information and strategies that are different, unexploited and unhyped and offer value that others haven't yet discovered. Not contrarian for the sake of it, and not innovative too early, you will make most of your profit from hidden-from-the-masses value. Using this philosophy, you will also gain from increases in the value of the asset once it enters the consciousness of the masses – often once the value of it has risen significantly and been hyped up by the media.

There are essentially five parts to the uncommon sense philosophy:

1 Have one-half of one eye on mainstream views and news.
2 Investigate and research for yourself by looking for information and strategies that are different, unexploited and unhyped and offer value that others haven't yet discovered.
3 Don't be contrarian for the sake of it.
4 Don't innovate too early.
5 Look for hidden-from-the-masses value.

1 Have half an eye on mainstream views and news

Some successful people have a 'no mass media' diet. While I understand why they want to stay positive and be unaffected by hypothesis and hyperbole, I feel it is important to stay in touch with current affairs. General news and politics affect stock and asset prices and also custom to your business. Therefore, they are an important part of business and investing. You just have to manage the correct dosage of each outlet, taking the credible ones seriously and taking the sensationalist ones with a pinch of salt. Later in this book, I'll share the publications I find most credible and useful and those that I tend to pass by. I have been asked many times to share this information.

2 Investigate and research for yourself

Look for information and strategies that are different, unexploited and unhyped and offer value that others haven't yet discovered.

Many successful businesspeople – like Walt Disney, Warren Buffett and James Caan – have followed the mantra of 'observe the masses, do the opposite'. This has now become more mainstream than it used to be because it has been popularized by people whose success has been vast enough to reach the mainstream, and also because of the current popularization of business and entrepreneurship with shows like *Dragons' Den* and *The Apprentice*. This will lead to point 3 below, but, for now, ensure that you take all mainstream media, commentary and advice with a pinch of salt. Do your own diligence and research, and educate yourself in niches that seem to be untapped and have inherent value.

3 Don't be contrarian for the sake of it

In order to not be contrarian for the sake of being contrarian, we need to define contrarianism. A contrarian is someone who rejects popular opinion or current practice, regardless of how popular it might be. I believe this to be a useful mindset and strategy for investing, business and finance, because the asset value is likely to be overpriced if everyone thinks it is good. Often when something is popular, many have already bought into the asset and there is a premium attached to the price. The greater the excitement in an asset class, the more 'froth' it has (airy matter with no substance). There is an excited expectation of the forward price, but without there being any real substance or value.

When the market turns, the froth evaporates fast and you find that the coffee you bought fills only half the cup, the froth taking with it a chunk of the value of your asset.

Because 'contrarianism' has become a concept in its own right, popularized by successful investors like Warren Buffett, or the perception of him, it has started to take on mainstream appeal. As soon as something can be 'defined', it can be copied and the masses inevitably flock in. The more exposure contrarianism gets, the less contrarian it becomes. This is a paradox and a reason why I am avoiding giving you a one-line quote or one-word name for my investment strategies. They are not holistic and cannot be simplified. Once labelled, they may be blindly followed and thus become less effective. By virtue of the fact that most business owners and investors are not successful for a sustained period of time, you will be doing the opposite of the masses, and that is as far as we should define it. So be contrarian because others don't and can't do what you can do – not just for the sake of it.

4 Don't innovate too early

It is true to say that you can be 'too early' in a business model or investment. If you had the idea for the Internet in 1695, you may have been burned at the stake. If your model or investment theory is too complicated, relies heavily on very advanced technology, or has great resistance from competitors, it may be best to put it on ice and wait.

There are some famous-but-didn't-become-famous examples of those who were too early. Remember 'Ask Jeeves', the search engine? The Go Corporation created the early palm pilots and tablets that Apple have leveraged so well. LetsBuyIt.com was Groupon before Groupon. LoudCloud was cloud computing before cloud computing.

Being the first, one of the first, or very early, of course, has the upside of there being less competition, more value and more room for growth, but it has the big risk downside of not being tested, proven, understood or scalable. You often hear only the wild success stories of the innovations that changed the world, and not the hundreds or thousands of failed cases. And, in fact, if you look at those wild successes, Facebook was not the first social media platform, Apple didn't produce the first phone, computer or music-sharing site, and eBay and Amazon were not the first online auction or retail sites. You are often best observing the 'version 2.0s'. Watch, sit on your hands for a while, learn and see how they develop and whether they can get through those hard early stages. Let them test and burn cash for you. Learn vicariously through their mistakes, and then get in once the concept has been proven and when the major risks and errors have mostly been removed.

5 Look for hidden-from-the-masses value

Value is latent profit, and so has not been fully extracted. By definition, it is hidden from the masses. How can you find those hidden gems? Can you look at a class in a different way? Can you look at a new class completely? Can you iterate a strategy that was nearly there but missed an essential ingredient or improvement? Can you look at a different field and bring existing models into your new field as a way of innovating without the risk?

I like to go running as it clears my mind and sets me up for a day of productive business and investing. When I run, and often while I am driving, I will take strategic detours in search of hidden properties. Maybe they are properties that have just come on the market and didn't have a 'for sale' board up yesterday. Maybe they are properties hidden behind trees that I didn't notice before. Maybe they are properties that have been defaced, that are in disrepair, have multiple 'for sale' boards outside, or are for lease. If I can spot these first, or more specifically, if I can spot the change of circumstances first, I may have found a hidden-from-the-masses asset, with value to be extracted and cashed in on.

> Follow these five guidelines that form the 'uncommon sense' philosophy and you will beat the popular misconceptions of business, investing and finance, and you will profit handsomely by going against the tide.

2

Business, investing and finance: how to profit by going against the tide

Writing isn't my natural flow. I often only end up writing articles and books when I'm asked so much that I know there is demand and I know I can add enough value to enough people. If I could summarize what I think about business, finance and investing that could be taught to others, it is that many people do not know what they are doing. So if I could add the most value to you, it would be in pointing out the plethora of these fallacies one by one, especially the popular, 'conventional wisdom' ones. I would bust those myths using my experience and then give you ideas and strategies to profit by going against them – things that make 'uncommon sense'.

Please note that I will be giving you my opinion formed from my experience in business and investing since my early teens. I am someone with a real passion and who has turned that passion into a profession. I do not profess to have all the answers. I have made mistakes (which I will openly share) and do not like to be labelled an expert, a guru, or any such term to make out that I know it all. This is not so much a disclaimer, though of course you should seek professional advice when investing, but more a statement that we are all learning all the time and should remain hungry students. A big part of the philosophy of uncommon sense is to enjoy discovering new opportunities that others can't find, and that is a never-ending (and exciting) pursuit.

Most of your latent profit exists in classes, niches and business models that others haven't discovered or fully leveraged. I will endeavour to help you unearth these. You will be tempted, lured and persuasively sold into classes and models aimed towards the masses, and this book is about how to spot and avoid these and profit by going against them.

This is not a book of specific investment advice. This is not a rehash of a Buffett, Munger, or Soros strategy. I hope that this book is one you can't define and fills a gap that stands the test of time rather than jumping on a fad, and it applies to all areas of business, finance and investing. There are fundamental but little-known concepts that occur in all cycles, markets and models. Whether they are presented in the same way or repackaged, these fundamental concepts are based on inherent human behaviour. This will be the focus of this book, because I believe in long-term, sustained wealth building and investing. Yes, you may make some flash-in-the pan, short-term arbitrage by going with the masses. If this is what you are looking for, this book may not be for you. Business, finance and investing are my highest passions and to that end I am very fortunate to have created a full-time career from monetizing my hobbies. And, because of that, short-term risks don't interest me.

My hope is that you grow year on year and leverage your previous investments in time, cash and knowledge, harnessing the benefits of momentum and compounding to build a fortress that no one can infiltrate. There will be constant and consistent attacks on your wealth in the form of taxes, critics, trolls, ex-partners, competitors and regulations. You will need this momentum to carry you through for the long term. Do not take instant-fix shortcuts that jeopardize long-term sustainability. Realize that, no matter what your age, you have much longer ahead and can be much more patient than you often realize. There is a saying that I like: 'Most people overestimate what they can achieve in a short time but underestimate what they can achieve in a lifetime.' When asked about his secrets to success, Buffett cited compounding and great genes as his two main success factors. So leverage consistent compounding for the long term, do not chop and change, and live a long and profitable life.

The uncommon sense mentality

I have a Polish contractor who has an 'enterprising' way of cementing and generating new business relationships. He has created a way to form connections with his customers and gain access to their networks to get more work. When a friend of mine (for whom this contractor was also doing some work) was about to get married, he offered to 'do the fireworks'. Little did we know what this meant!

He turned up to the event with a lorry and two men. They approached the next-door neighbour's house to ask if they could set the fireworks off from her garden. As the wedding was being held on the peninsula of the biggest artificial lake in Europe, there was plenty of room for these fireworks to go off. The homeowner naturally hesitated at the idea of ash and flames potentially going over her manicured lawn, so he used some uncommon sense. Pushing his hand in his pocket, he pulled out £50 and offered it as a fee to use the lawn. Since the property must have been worth around £3 million, she looked a little embarrassed and said, 'Oh no, we couldn't possibly take that,' and promptly agreed to let him use the garden. It seemed that the mere offer of the fee had pushed her into agreeing. Within minutes, three Polish men were in her garden setting up what can only be described as imported Polish munitions.

As the night drew in the fireworks started. The wedding guests were amazed at the display, which was probably as big as that in London during the millennium celebrations. Many of them ask to meet the builder and he made numerous connections that resulted in several million pounds' worth of building projects for him. He had done what others wouldn't or didn't know how to: he pushed the boundaries, knocked on doors, and didn't take no for an answer to create an extravaganza. This is very much the uncommon sense mentality – though in this case perhaps a little rough around the edges.

3

The signs that the lemmings are about to walk off the cliff

There are consistent telltale signs that the masses are moving blindly in droves. When you begin to recognize and understand these behaviour patterns, take it as a sign that you should sit on your hands or go against the tide. It is important to set these out early: while the loudest voices often have the biggest impact on the movement of the masses, they are also most often the most wrong.

Tighten your belt and guard your capital against the following:

1 Your friend or the shoeshine giving you advice on stocks

This is a sure sign there are too many people in the market and the probability of a big fall is higher. This is rather crudely known as 'dumb money'. Be very wary when people with no experience or, worse, people who've previously shown no interest in an asset class are giving out free advice.

2 Stocks performing with consistently high growth for many years

The best time to get value in an asset class is during bare, lean times. Yet this is not a draw for the masses. The masses respond to consistent proven growth, and this is common sense. All this track record does is make it easy for an IFA or investment adviser to sell, which opens the floodgates for the masses. The longer proven gains have occurred, the wider the news of this travels, and the more unsophisticated investors rush to invest. Over time, this pushes the price up and the value, equity or margin down. The market is in constant flux between lagging and slow to price in gains, or overpricing value. It rarely finds equilibrium, and often the momentum from the upswing of gains is inevitably followed by a rapid fall.

3 Investment funds advertised on a London bus and taxi

Advertisers will pick out a fund that has performed well over the last few years and show you the returns historically because it is the easiest fund to sell. This is done by plastering ads on buses, the Tube and anywhere advertisers can buy space. The common perception is that, if a fund has performed well over one, three or five years, then it is a good fund to buy. This is often wrong. And when so much money can be pumped into mainstream advertising to create a buzz, this often means that the returns are not only unrealistically high but they are also unsustainable. This manufactured high may not last much longer and is very likely to be 'priced in' (overpriced).

4 Hotspots being promoted and pumped

The public are wooed by the next upcoming hotspot talk and are easy to sell to. Like a consistently well-performing stock, if prices have been strong for many years, you are probably too late to the party and the inherent value is mostly gone. Everyone loves the thought of cashing in on a goldmine hotspot area, and the average investor will fall for the same few marketable amenities:

- 'Crossrail is coming in five years.'
- 'Once Crossrail is here, there'll be huge demand for renters and London commuter homeowners, which will force growth.'
- 'The Olympics are coming.'

In the run-up to the Olympics in 2012, Stratford became the new hotspot. Many new-build flats were constructed in the area to meet this perceived future demand. The pundits were pumping it. As with all hotspots, the growth gets forward-priced into the new-builds by the developers because the glitz and allure of the quick profit makes them so easy to sell. The masses are drawn in, convinced of the ease of selling these properties. Before you know it, the momentum from their movement has swing and the prices shoot up further. Only those who got in right at the start, when it wasn't getting hyped up, make sustained profits. Seeing the prices skyrocket with the mass movement in, these early investors cash in by getting out, thus profiting by going against the tide.

5 Making overseas 'holiday home investments'

'Invest in a holiday home, spend the summer there and rent it out for the rest of the year' is the spiel. However, it only rents out for a few weeks (or months if you are lucky) of the year. The only times you want to stay in it are during peak season and other times of the year when others want to rent it too. You have paid top, new-build, priced-in money for it, too – if it ever got built, that is. Brits love property and love a holiday home investment opportunity even more. The idea of a place overseas in the sun, preferably near a beach, are all so easy to sell to the English, especially if mortgages are easy to get. I discuss the 'priced-in' concept in more detail in coming chapters. If something is far away, difficult to understand, new and overpriced, but ticks all the boxes for an emotional sale, it is likely to lure in the lemmings. I speak from personal experience here, and if you have read my previous book, *Low Cost High Life*, you will remember my experiences with Bansko in Bulgaria and other overseas investments.

6 Low rates

When rates are low, it creates false confidence. This is because the real, longer-term, average cost of finance hasn't been factored in. Sure, low rates are better for cash flow, but you have to act as if these low rates are a transient moment in time and not the norm. This especially affects car purchases. If people are earning no money in a savings account, they'd rather it earn more in something they can see and touch. This means real asset classes, but sometimes people buy cars by convincing themselves that it's also an asset, because prices have 'accidentally' gone up without requiring due dilligence or skill. However, many people buy cars to appease their ego; nothing pleases them more than showing them off. When prices of normally highly depreciative new cars are firm, as they were in 2016 when many newish, non-limited-run Ferraris and Porsches went up in value, be wary.

4

When it's easy to sell, it may smell

The easier an investment class or business model is to sell, the more allure it has for the masses. This is not to say that something that is easy to sell never works, but just that there are consistent attributes that may end up devaluing the asset or business. For example, an easy investment can attract too many unsophisticated investors or too many competitors, both of which reduce the margin.

Common attributes that make an investment easy to sell include religion, culture and habits or beliefs that are ingrained in the national psyche. A big one is emotion; think of how a child pulls at the strings of a parent. For example, the love a mother has for her child makes her spend £300 on a pushchair. Another common one is sex; we all know sex sells just about anything. While I can't imagine how a billboard with the sign 'Buy now' plastered across Eva Herzigova's underwear would be a persuasive strategy for the latest fund, these common sales tactics are worth a brief mention so you can spot them and avoid them. Are you buying in on the fundamentals or are your emotional strings or long-held beliefs being pulled at?

Resisting the easy sells

Specific to the uncommon sense philosophy and to profiting by going against the tide, here are some business, finance and investing signs that indicate when something is easy to sell, and therefore may smell:

1 Proven market outperforming growth

The longer a market has had unsustainably high returns, the less likely it is that you can buy with inherent value or the ability to add value. The more mature a business is, the harder it is to get in and sustain a good profit margin. A good indicator of this will be ads and investment professionals showing these consistent returns as a gauge of what will likely happen in the future. The uncommon sense reality is that the longer the market has sustained outperforming market growth, the closer to a correction it most likely is.

2 Social proof (endorsements by celebrities or the masses)

This can be linked to the indicator above and, in addition, as soon as you see lots of big, unrelated celebrity endorsements, or an angle that 'everyone is doing it, so you should too', it is a sign that prices and profits may be unsustainable.

3 The mass media popularizing an asset class

This includes classes that people inherently love anyway, for example the idea that the English love property and that many people from the Middle East love gold. When a model or class is already ingrained in the national psyche, it provides a fertile ground for emotional salesmanship. If a class or model is popularized in the tabloid press, it is time to put the uncommon sense hat on and stick to the philosophy, despite the pressure from the masses.

4 Ease of finance (and low cost)

When finance is free flowing and anyone can get a loan or mortgage, the markets are never far away from correcting. The better things become for a sustained time period, the more the perils of the past are forgotten and the more money is thrown at people who may not have been previously loan-worthy. This is done to hit quotas and market share and to match lending volumes from competitors. There was a loan humorously known as a NINJA loan towards the peak before the recession of 2007: the 'No Income, No Job, no Assets loan'. When loan to values get too high, when banks are too willing to lend, and when people you know shouldn't borrow money seem to be getting it for free, take heed and proceed with caution.

5 Emotional pulls

Holiday home investments, life insurances that scare you to death, and products sold by pulling on your parental heartstrings are all easy sells. We may justify them later, after the purchase, with some loose logic.

6 New/tech/first

If something is the first, it is easily marketable as the next big thing, the first thing to take the market by storm. This is especially easy to do and a sucker punch in the tech world. Everything is the next Facebook or hyped as the Uber of a new niche – except that this rarely, if ever, happens. Companies like Amazon and Google are very uncommon, so don't be lured by the popular dramatization. People often ask me what I would do if I could go back and start my business all over again. I tell them that, with the benefit of hindsight, I would buy all Facebook and Google stock at the start. If only it were that easy.

7 Scarcity

'You need to be fast, take action now or you will lose out.' We all get sucked into that common scarcity tactic. Apple, for example, use this fear of missing out to create such a buzz that people will queue for days for a new phone launch. Be aware of your emotions and, when you feel pulled to make a snap decision, ask yourself whether you are acting on logic and analysis or the fear of missing out.

8 Hyperbole

'Buy to let is dead (prices are down 5 or 10 per cent).' 'Buy to let is booming (prices are up 5 per cent).' 'The stock market has crashed (dropped 5 per cent).' The media hypes and sensationalizes information to sell newspapers, creating polarized extremes that are usually exaggerated in either direction. Reality is generally far less extreme and exciting, so always assume this and see through the hyperbole.

To reiterate, I am not giving a judgement call that all selling is bad. In fact, as long as what you are saying is true, it is smart to use some of these proven strategies to sell good products and services in your business. My aim here is to make you aware of what you are going into, to be able to isolate what is emotion and what is logic. This is a crucial skill that will allow you make the investment decisions that will give you the best and most sustainable returns.

5

'Priced in' and 'real value'

When the general, perceived wisdom is that something is likely to rise in value in the future, then more people invest or buy in, becoming a part of the increase in value. This, in turn, pushes it beyond its 'real value'. Another theory or similar phenomenon is described by George Soros as 'reflexivity':

> In economics, reflexivity refers to the self-reinforcing effect of market sentiment, whereby rising prices attract buyers whose actions drive prices higher still until the process becomes unsustainable and the same process operates in reverse leading to a catastrophic collapse in prices. This is an instance of a positive feedback loop.
>
> Wikipedia, 'Reflexivity (social theory)'

Any upside potential has largely gone, due to the price already reacting to expectation. 'Expectation theory' is where things become what they are expected to become, rather than what the fundamentals, rationale or information would have them be. They never achieve equilibrium based on their merits and investments effectively become a self-fulfilling prophecy.

A great example of this occurred in 2016. Most finance houses suggested that the value of the pound would drop by around 15 per cent if the UK voted to leave the European Union. That is exactly what happened the very next morning. This shift was not created because the UK capital account had materially changed overnight; instead, it was largely down to the general expectation that this shift would occur, and that interest rates would need to fall to loosen monetary policy in a bid to stave off recession.

Emotion, fear, greed, mass movement and momentum all affect prices and push them up or down. In the event of overconfidence, you have an asset value that is forward priced (worth a future price with an existing lag) owing to the expectation and reflexivity of the masses and the market. 'Real value' is where there is none of this 'froth' or, even better, there is a lack of confidence and 'reverse' reflexivity or the expectation of a bare outlook. This also affects the price in the opposite direction to 'priced in', and is often a prime time to buy in or start an enterprise.

Equilibrium is the price that an asset reaches when supply and demand of the asset are equally matched. This is a rare occurrence, as emotions of fear and greed drive the equilibrium closer to the outer extremes.

Part 2: Popular misconceptions

In this section I will detail some uncommon sense ideas and then dig into the mistakes that I and others have made to extract the valuable lessons that reduce risk and increase profit. Learning from our own mistakes and the mistakes of others allows us to create leverage and benefit from things that have gone wrong. Contrary to popular belief that the best lessons are taught through mistakes and experience, I believe that the cheapest lessons are those you learn vicariously through the mistakes of others. That is the theme of this section and my goal for you.

6

Most assets make no money

This is true, I'm afraid – for the masses, at least. Most assets make no money. Most property makes no money. Most stocks lose money. Most cars lose money. Most watches lose money. You get the picture. People think generically and universally that an investment class either makes money, or it doesn't. They subscribe to the idea that a business model is a goldmine or a money pit.

The reality is that any class can make money, but only a specific sub- or super-niche of that class: a niche that is well known, researched and experienced. I'll give an example in a moment, but first we need to be clear on what an asset is. In my interpretation, an asset is anything that has value. Significant assets, to my mind, should appreciate in value and often provide an income. I would argue (unlike some commentators) that your own home is a significant asset. In the UK, homes are likely to increase in value over time at a higher rate than the interest on the mortgage used to purchase it.

When making investments, cash flow and net income are the two most important things to focus on. They keep you and the investment safe during more difficult times and are what you can live off. A liability is anything that has a net negative value or something that cash-flows negatively. As cash flow is the only real thing that kills businesses, it needs to be watched like a hawk and special attention should be made to find and focus on assets with positive cash flows.

Understanding sub-niches

Let's look at a working example of a sub-niche of an asset: watches. My guess is that most people don't see watches as an investment class. However, others with a basic knowledge of investing concepts may believe that they are a great investment class. I've never seen mainstream watches rise in value. The most obviously mainstream of the non-mainstream is Rolex. So those with a limited knowledge think that Rolex watches are a good investment. But they are wrong: most Rolexes do not appreciate in value; in fact, virtually all women's Rolexes depreciate. In addition to this, virtually all Rolex dress watches depreciate; the same is true of almost all their standard-issue watches, which depreciate with time. It's only really the 'sports models' that appreciate, but not all of them. And among the ones that do gain value, they all depreciate first. The only exception would be a very rare special run or limited edition, but those are not easily accessible, even to a dedicated collector or investor.

I am not writing this section to intentionally confuse, but to illustrate what it takes to understand a niche. I am by no means a watch expert. However, the thought process that I am explaining can be applied to virtually any asset class or business model.

You hear that 'sports Rolexes' appreciate. You do some research and find out that these sports models are Sea-Dwellers, Deepsea Dwellers, Submariners and Daytonas. On further investigation, you find that these models are crafted in steel, white gold, yellow gold, rose gold and platinum. They can be created with an assortment of gems and various straps. Then you discover the release of a new sports model called the Sky Dweller. Is this in the 'Sports Rolex' category? Your research reveals that the gold versions mostly seem to drop in value, but were strong in 2016. However, some of the old pre-1980s gold Daytonas fetch 800 per cent more than the 2016/17 retail price, 1,400 per cent more than their new price. So is a gold sports Rolex a good investment or not? You research further and find the nearly new prices of the gold Sky Dweller are selling at 60 per cent of retail. So maybe steel is better? If you research the price of the Deepsea Dweller, you will notice that the second-hand prices are 65 per cent of the new price. But that is only post-2014, as the prices were firmer after the 2007/08 recession. Back to this in a minute...

At this point, you've now worked out that second hand seems to be better value than new. But is that watch coming from a private seller who has worn it as their main watch or a collector who has kept it in a safe? Perhaps the seller is a dealer who can offer a warranty and history/paperwork with the watch? There are more considerations, such as which country should you buy it in. This could depend on the state of the currency and the possible arbitrage against other currencies. As it turns out, it could be all of these, or any, or none, depending on condition, price, model and so on. Is it better to pay a higher price but have the box and paperwork and receipt, or a lower price but no proof of purchase (missing receipt, box, paperwork, or all three)?

And if a limited edition comes out, like the James Cameron Deepsea 'Deep Blue', or a new version of a model like the Platinum Daytona, should you wait until they are second hand to hope for a lower price, or buy them new because they will have a premium attached to them? If there is a very limited edition like a sports model only for the special forces and the price seems to have a premium already attached, should you buy new or wait for a collector to sell, if they ever will?

You ask yourself these questions as you research previous Rolex sports models. Take, for example, the 'Single Red' and the 'Double Red' Sea-Dwellers. The 'Single Red' has risen steadily, but not dramatically, and the 'Double Red' has risen more, especially in the few years leading to 2015/16. Perhaps you believe that you can invest in variations, short runs or novelty sports Rolexes. At first glance, these seem to be a good bet. But on further investigation you learn that there are hundreds of variations in terms of model numbers, serial numbers/codes attached to the year, dial, mark and so on (Rolex do not publish production volumes).

The more you niche, the more you discover; you quickly learn that as the sports Rolex ages, the 'patina' (variance of dial fade) becomes important. It is crucial that the piece is unmolested (not polished, no parts replaced, even if they are part worn or slightly damaged), and sometimes the heritage (who owned it before and its backstory) of the piece can have a huge impact on its valuation.

If you are still with me, then we have culled 95 per cent of the people looking for a fast and easy recommendation that they can 'bet' on. It excites me to go to these lengths to get a level of understanding and knowledge that other people don't have or can't stay the distance to discover. I hope it is just as exciting for you. For this reason, I think it is important to get into models and classes you enjoy. This is sustainable and ensures you get maximum enjoyment and leverage out of the work-life balance quandary. Later in this chapter, I will discuss the three options you have for investing in different asset classes.

> If you can merge your passion and profession, vocation and vacation,
> then you are doing what you would do as a hobby, but you get to make
> a living (maybe even a fortune) out of it.
>
> Rob Moore

To summarize, if you are looking to invest in watches, and as an analogy for all other classes of investment, you need to weigh up all the factors such as new versus second hand, where you buy second hand, heritage and history, proof and warranty, material, past residuals, novelties, patina, dials, condition, supply, materials and their inherent value, demand, market conditions, currency and location, popularity and celebrity endorsement, and brand. Only after these factors have been carefully considered do you make a decision to buy and hold, buy and flip, or wait.

When you break this down, out of the million or more watches that Rolex make in a year, perhaps only a few thousand will appreciate in value in the long run – perhaps fewer than 5 per cent. This is also true of the number of houses in a given area that will serve as a good investment, despite almost every house increasing in capital value year on year, as proven through history. It is also the same in terms of the number of paintings that are sold that will appreciate and the number of stock-market investments that will steadily and sustainably rise. It is also true of the number of businesses that will succeed beyond three, five or ten years.

Do not let this put you off. It is simply the entrance fee into your niche or class. It is a gatekeeper to filter out most of your competition and it makes success easier the longer you stay in the game. The knowledge that in every asset class most of the investments do not pay is something that will help you focus on the uncommon sense philosophy and methodology of searching for investments away from the mass hysteria – like the old Rolexes that look subtle and nondescript yet have proven and sustainable residuals, and like the dirty, ugly properties that put other people off. (It's also like the unsexy tobacco companies that give great returns over the long term – although you can make your own ethical decision about choosing this type of investment.)

Monetizing assets: a case study

Most assets make no money, but the few that do, do it consistently. The problem is that most people do not know what they are or how to monetize them.

As we moved into the industry of providing courses and seminars, it became clear that we would need to transport and carry all the speakers, pop-ups and other necessary equipment to and from hotels. Since the credit crunch had started, I noticed that Range Rovers had plummeted in value and that the petrol versions were especially cheap. I thought it would be uncommon sense to buy what everyone wanted to sell. While I knew that the petrol version was very cheap, there were LPG converted versions around for not much more money, and much cheaper than the diesel versions. In the end, we bought the LPG version since the cost to run one is significantly less than diesel. It seemed logical to give the car to our property buyer for weekday viewings, and on the weekend seminar days we could pack it full of gear to take to the next hotel.

It was not the most reliable car we had ever bought. One afternoon, we had parked it in Peterborough outside the office in a pedestrian precinct to load it up for a major event we were running. The plan was to drive and unload it that evening ready for the next day. However, when we came to start it, the battery was flat. It was 7 p.m. on a Friday evening. We frantically called the AA and they offered to be there in four hours. The team started to become despondent.

I remembered a chap who ran a local backstreet garage. He had serviced my Nova for £25 and was always very accommodating. I gave him a call and 20 minutes later a lad had arrived and started work on the car. The street was busy and traffic wardens and police were starting to circle, delivery drivers were not able to get through and pedestrians were becoming irate. Shouting a few words, the mechanic got back in his 1987 Nissan Micra and steamed off to the parts shop. He arrived back shortly afterwards with a new battery. He quickly fitted it and offered his oil-spattered hand to shake mine. His boss came on the phone requesting a £27 payment – £27 to attend on site at 8 p.m. on a Friday and supply and fit a new Range Rover battery. To me, it was uncommon sense to use my backstreet contact: we were able to get something done quickly that a slicker, well-marketed operation that most people would have gone to couldn't – and for much less money.

(Three years later we sold the Range Rover for exactly what we had paid for it, so it effectively just cost us the maintenance for the period we owned it.)

> As the subtitle of this book states, I believe in profiting by going against the tide. I don't do this for the sake of it, but seemingly by nature and by observing popular misconceptions so as to avoid them. I don't see this as a negative but as a great lesson. What do others do wrong that you can learn from? The truth is that most people don't make good, sustained investments or business decisions, and so by looking to their failures we can find an abundance of lessons in what not to do. After all, if everyone were successful, there would be no 'successful', or at least successful would become average.

7

'Alternative' investments

Many 'alternative' investments that regularly arise show some common threads that you will want to avoid like the plague. These are common misconceptions because ordinary folk fall for them hook, line and sinker. Much like 'alternative' medicine, they are inherently risky and unproven. Not only are many of these investments unregulated, but they are also often designed by people who know that the few early adopters or 'people at the top of the pyramid' will reap the largest rewards, leaving very little or nothing for the average investors beneath them. They promise unrealistically high returns and are often billed as easy pickings with little to no time investment. I see it as my duty to educate and warn you of these, so you can quickly spot the signs and save yourself wasted time and capital. While on very rare occasion one might take off, this is so unlikely as to be not worth mentioning.

While I have no fear of naming the specific alternative products that prove my case and went 'smelly', I will not name the culprits because I am more interested in you spotting the type of investment rather than specific past schemes.

Here are the most common flash-in-the-pan, fly-by-night 'investments':

1 Most multi-level marketing (MLM)

MLM is a marketing strategy in which the sales force is compensated not only for the sales that they personally make but also for the sales that recruited participants make. This is also known as the 'down line'.

Using MLM or affiliate-based products can be a good grounding for learning how to sell. When MLM is wrapped around the right product, all the downsides actually strengthen the skills and character of the salesperson. They harden their ability to take rejection and receive resistance. They benefit from the supportive atmosphere of a community and really earning every sale. Enduring positive examples that seem to work include Tupperware, Avon, Herbalife and Utility Warehouse. With many products, however, the referral or down-line element of the MLM model makes it all too easy to build and sell an MLM system based purely on the 'pyramid' rather than on the strength of the product. This is when it gets into scam territory.

Many pyramid schemes package themselves as MLM but sell on the promise of income with no work, rather than on the strength of the sales and quality of the product. Emphasis is put on the recruitment of the down-line sales force rather than the strength of the product in these types of pyramid schemes. In these schemes, where the pyramid is dressed up as MLM, people are not buying in on the basis of the strength of the product but for the promise of pumped-up returns with little effort, all earned by your up and down line. Although they are illegal in China, in the United States there are over 1,000 legal and well-run MLM companies. Pyramid schemes, however, are banned in the United States.

The main difference between an MLM and a pyramid scheme is that MLMs have a real product to sell to the general public, and do not require consumers to spend money to join the MLM system. MLMs pay a commission to distributors but these commissions are real sales and not necessarily new recruits. Pyramids, when dressed up as MLMs, can survive and thrive because it is not immediately clear to participants or authorities that people are signing up to receive rewards from signing others up rather than from utilizing the product.

An exotic Tahitian drink is made from the fruit of a rare tree that is indigenous to South-East Asia. The fruit and the tree shall remain nameless. This mysterious juice has been promoted as a cure for a number of different diseases. In 2004 the US Food and Drug Administration issued a warning against the company that makes the juice, for making unfounded health claims with no scientific evidence to prove any health benefits. This was a classic pyramid dressed up as an MLM scheme, and you need to be aware that there are many others like it currently doing the rounds.

2 Web traffic generation/referral links/click revenue

There have been many schemes related to web traffic generation, referral links and click revenue. Some of these schemes have been shut down by the authorities; some have had their founders imprisoned. They are based on clicking banners, paying for web tracking, referral link generation, or clicking on ads repeatedly. Many are hard to understand because the flow of money is unclear, which makes them more worthy of scam status and provides another warning sign.

Never go into a business model or investment if you don't understand the mechanics of it. You are more vulnerable to have your brain baffled and to have to rely on your emotions or intuition because you can't reason with clarity or grasp the concept. Many schemes seem intentionally vague for this reason, and increasingly, if I can't grasp the concept clearly and quickly, I don't even bother trying.

3 Carbon credits

Many companies have sold or purported to sell investments in carbon credits – the latest magic pill of renewable energy, sustainability and tax write-offs. The companies selling these investments to unsophisticated investors latch on to sensitive and emotive subjects like climate change and leverage them to sell investments in an otherwise well-intentioned exchange of carbon emissions allowances. These are usually not sustainable investments, but more a flash-in-the-pan opportunity for the opportunistic entrepreneur.

4 Forestry

Forestry is another investment that profits off the back of green and sustainable energy. You may be cold-called and encouraged to engage in a pension review. Then, as part of the selling technique, forestry will be advertised as part of a proposed new pension plan. You 'invest' in forestry, teak, bamboo, forestry shares, tree plantations and Christmas trees. As if that isn't a warning enough, you are often told that you are in the early stages of the investment, and that, as the trees grow, are harvested and sold, you will generate a several-fold return on your investment. Last year, according to Action Fraud, 26 per cent of victims who reported investment scams had invested in unregulated forestry investments.

This is similar to a past scheme involving investing in ostrich eggs. Rates of return up to 270 per cent were promised if you invested. It was claimed that these eggs would become a popular source of food and the breeding of the birds would be wildly profitable. In just 15 months, £21 million was taken in from 2,800 customers. It was later discovered that 900 of the company's ostriches didn't exist, and that much of the money had been diverted into offshore accounts.

5 Hotel rooms

The companies that sell hotel rooms build or buy a hotel, and then often sell the rooms on at a very high margin. Thus the rooms are overvalued for the purchaser. They will buy on a higher return/yield, and then sell on to retail investors at a yield/return that is lower but still acceptable to them, creating a big capital uplift. What the retail investors don't understand is that they have made large capital losses immediately after purchase because they are buying on yield/return without understanding the capital element. If you include that in your overall return, you often end up with a negative return. You'd need years of high income to recoup the capital loss and hope that you get future capital increases high enough to make up the initial capital drop.

This is also how people get lured into overseas 'holiday home' investments, because of a lack of understanding of the local capital values. You need to factor in the capital as well as income returns in your overall return.

6 Electronic currency

There have been investments that are 'electronic currencies' or precious metals. To be clear, I am not talking about currencies like Bitcoin, but other e-currencies that are supposedly backed by precious metals. There have been cases where the US government has totally shut down these operations, causing all the money to disappear in a cloud of smoke. Poof. Gone.

7 Land investments

Someone buys up a field, carves it up into smaller lots, and persuades investors that there is a high probability that they will get planning permission and that then the value will soar. In reality, most of the land is agricultural with little or no chance of getting planning permission. A quick call to the local planning department will confirm this. Many investors have paid prices equivalent to land that already had planning consent on it. In reality, there was no reasonable prospect of obtaining planning permission and so the value of the land was little more than the value of agricultural land.

8 Holiday homes

Own an amazing second home in the sun, live in it for three months of the year and then make loads of money renting it out for the rest of the year. But the dream rarely matches reality: sometimes the properties don't even get built, and, if they are, the prices are highly inflated because overseas investors have no idea of the real values. In addition, the place in the sun is rarely what you need for your holiday, with few amenities and poor-quality finishing, and is therefore also difficult to rent out.

The bigger resellers of holiday homes often pay out huge commissions to affiliates, resellers and financial advisers. The costs of these commissions are added to the purchase price, which further inflates the price to the buyer. It is a good rule of thumb that the bigger the brochure, the more you should take heed.

9 Copycats

Once a new scheme appears that seems to have all the allure and traits mentioned in these examples, you get copycats flooding the market looking for a quick and easy win. You will often see the same thing repackaged over and over so as to look new or different. Once you have seen one of them, you have mostly seen them all.

Of course, I have made some generalizations in this section. But I have done so based on real and specific experiences and observations. Keep your eyes open and you will start to see these patterns all around you. If it looks like a duck, swims like a duck and quacks like a duck, then it probably is a duck. If the alternative starts to become mainstream and common, it is time to profit by going against the tide in a real asset class.

8

Who is already 'investing'?

I tend to look at who is doing the 'alternative' investment, or indeed any investment, as a quick guide to its validity. I can usually work out within a nanosecond whether it is likely to be a good investment based purely on who else is involved with it. If someone has been in a model or class for many years, has proven success, is well respected, withstands due diligence and has a good reputation, then I am keen to learn from, partner with, hire or even be mentored by this person. Like the uncommon sense philosophy and profiting by going against the tide, these people are not common and not easy to find on the high street or in the local pub. If and when you find them, hold on to them, stay close to them, employ them, pay them and partner with them. You may have only a handful of truly great people in your life, so play the long game and keep them.

And then, of course, there are plenty of people who do not fit with your vision. I would love for this to be a fluffy personal development book so I could tell you that everyone is great in their own way, everyone does the best they can with what they know, and that there is good in everyone. However, my sceptical nature forces me to warn you that, while of course some people are well intentioned, many others are more interested in your money than in a long-term partnership.

There are two main types of people who seem to leapfrog from one 'alternative' investment to another:

- **Type one** is simply naive.

This person is inexperienced; maybe they have just come out of a job, not had much business or investment experience, or they may be at a life decision crossroads. They need to move from this crossroads to improve a pain point in their life, which makes them susceptible and gives them 'happy eyes and ears'. They want and need to believe the unrealistic claims. They create justifications and defend the downside risks to themselves and others, even when those with more experience try to make them see more clearly and less emotionally.

- **Type two** is the perennial, serial scheme-peddler.

When you Google the names of the individuals or the schemes, you will often see the same people linked with selling the same new scams. They are like flies on a dungheap and this is their strategically chosen business model. If most investors are lemmings, then these scheme-peddlers are chameleons, changing the scheme they are promoting more often than their underwear. Although they would never admit it, I can only conclude that they know their scheme is a scam but believe that they will somehow be able to extract money out of it. They will draw in family, friends and existing customers who are ignorant of or indifferent to the consequences. You often see these people moving from country to country because a) they have to run away from those whom they've sucked in, and b) they need a new set of people to draw into the next scheme.

I have my suspicions that many of these type-two people have some kind of personality defect. It is as if they are missing the gene for empathy and remorse; they seem to feel no pain or guilt for the losses suffered by the people they brought in. They simply walk away and start again, like the snake-oil salesmen of old. I sometimes wonder whether they enjoy, or are even addicted to, the newness and dreamy hope that the next thing could be *the* big thing – or maybe that's just part of their sales spiel. I find it hard to understand their mentality because, to me, it makes more sense and is more sustainable to be in a model that builds goodwill, has longevity and serves people by providing real value for their money.

Identifying the scammers

In the last decade, I have met some interesting characters who might seem quite funny and likable if they hadn't sneakily pilfered and scammed money from people. I have found some common threads, which I now rely on before entering into partnerships or investments. I'll make three generalizations for ease of communication but, of course, just like great people, scammers come in all forms.

The 'charitable' scammer

The first type is the person who relies too much on their charity or religious credentials as a means of gaining the trust of others. Organizing charity events and giving to charity is great when it is done with the right intention and a genuine desire to help. However, don't be blinded by this seemingly selfless activity. The credibility, knowledge and track record of the person behind these activities are still important factors to consider. There is nothing wrong with people who are very religious or those who do a lot for charity, but don't assign blind trust to people simply because they are involved with charitable activities. There seems to be a common belief that these people are somehow more competent, too. My advice is to treat them just like anyone else; get to know them and perform the same checks as you would with anyone else.

The 'excitable' scammer

Another type of person to watch out for is the highly excitable type who pumps people up with their passion and emotion and then leverages this energy to move them into certain investments. These people usually lack business experience, have no real investment knowledge and are sometimes allied to MLM schemes. Detail, real knowledge and experience are often irrelevant to them; they often prefer to operate by the mantra 'Bullshit baffles brains'. Prizing hubris over all else, these people often prosper on the crest of the wave, right at the end of each macroeconomic cycle. However, when the tide goes out during downturns, it is clear that they are swimming naked. These people want you to avoid logic and reason. They push the 'You can research for ever but that won't make you any money' mantra.

In the past, these excitable types have accused me of being a procrastinator. In my early investing days I felt pressure from these people but, as with all these types, they become easier to spot as you gain experience. I now steer away before I even need to give them a response. I remember one such individual who gave a talk at a seminar. He walked forcefully on stage, took the microphone, and with a scrunched-up face blurted out as his opening line: 'I want to tell you right now that this is *not a scam*. I repeat, this is *not* a scam.' Well, at least I now knew it *was* a scam!

The 'carey-sharey-lovey' scammer

The final type is the 'carey-sharey-lovey' type. I have met a few people who have used a caring image to elicit trust from others and make them feel they don't need to go through the normal channels of diligence. The 'caring' types often make a point of their family and ethical credentials, too. These are commonly known as the three Cs: Charity, Church and Children. Reliance on this type of talk is a red flag. A genuine person will stand on their own merits and let their results speak for them.

We all operate by our own ethics. I believe that those who shout too loudly about their own, call others rogues or state how 'ethical' they are, are often in the business of misdirection. They point at everything and everyone but themselves, because they don't want you to scrutinize them too much. Their patter is usually nothing more than a sales technique that interrupts the logic centre of your brain. Often highly hypocritical, these people usually end up proving themselves to be anything but trustworthy and honest.

9

A note on trust and scepticism

You may have gathered by now that I like to be sure about something before I go into it. This seems the right time to discuss how trusting or sceptical we should be in business, finance and investing. Firstly, I believe it is important to approach new ideas with an open mind when they are presented by good sources. The mind is like a parachute: it generally works better when open. Being too sceptical or dismissive in the early stages of a new opportunity is likely to put off the person who is presenting the opportunity. It is also likely to reduce your ability to objectively assess it. Your gut will become very useful in guiding you when presented with new ideas. It is also healthy for your wellbeing to trust people who do not pose any threat to your wealth or business, so there is no need to be sceptical of everything anyone discusses in harmless or fun social environments.

Clearly, if the opportunity involves you placing a large amount of money, business or time into something that has little track record of independently verifiable success, you should be cautious. Many (but not all) people will try to convince you of anything and everything when they have your business and your money in their crosshairs. Watch out for investment opportunities that include a conflict of interest. Scenarios often arise where it is actually in the best interests of the provider to delay or fail to provide results, unless, of course, further revenue is due or payment is deferred until delivery.

Once the opportunity has passed the 'sniff test', it is a good idea to test it on a small, de-risked scale to prove and document the results. It is wise to do this regardless of how much you trust or are sceptical of the business, model or individual. No seasoned investor or entrepreneur will take your due diligence personally; they will recognize it as simply smart business. After all, things may have worked in the past but that is no guarantee of the future, and things may have worked for someone else but may not work for you. There are many hidden variables that are based not on one's credibility or honesty but on commercial reality.

You also have to value your time as well as your capital. Be aware of the time cost associated with every opportunity. A bargain in terms of financial cost does not necessarily come cheap. Do your research and ensure that it is not going to be a significant time drain. Once concept or investment has been proven, it can be rolled out and scaled according to the model created.

Trust, but always verify

In the workplace, and in business in general, it's important to be able to trust your staff and partners. How else can you get on with what you are doing, let others manage your systems, and allow your business to scale? However, it is important to verify the information being passed to you periodically (and apparently randomly). Whether it is with specific key performance indicators (KPIs) or other data spot checks, make sure that you are on the same page with the person doing the doing and ensure that they are performing the task in a way that benefits the wider goals of the business. Try to walk in their shoes for a day, do the things that they do, so that you can better understand their role. This will have multiple benefits. When you work alongside a person, you form a better relationship and understanding of them. In addition, you are likely to be able to better manage them and verify what they do. You will know at a glance whether they are performing the role correctly and whether you are being told something that is correct.

People will often self-preserve and so, without KPIs and other data sets, they may cover things up to protect themselves. I used to take what I perceived to be lies much more personally, but now I realize that these omissions and lies are not personal at all. They are not about you: they are mostly about the self-preservation of the other person. Another benefit of KPIs and data is that they are hard facts and so leave less room for manipulation of the truth.

In the early days of Progressive Property we had (and still have) some brilliant staff. One of our earlier property buyers used to get some extremely cheap property deals. Always out and about in the car doing viewings, he was a rather elusive character. The cheap deals kept rolling in, often 30 per cent plus below the market value, so we at HQ were happy. As time went on, though, it became clear that almost all the deals were coming from female agents, mainly located 'out in the sticks'. As time went on and he bought more properties, I noticed that a whole string of these women were dotted about his 'milk round'. Clearly, he had embraced the uncommon sense mentality and it was working well for him. We saw some of the ramifications of this with time.

Later on that year, it became clear that he he had used the same emotional tactics on a female colleague. She ended up moving roles and chose to depart not long afterwards. This is *not* the uncommon sense philosophy and *not* the reputation we wanted to build as a company of substance. I bit my tongue and dealt with the issue professionally but the damage within the business was done. I had definitely let the situation go on for too long without intervening. The lesson here is that it is good to trust, but always verify.

Creating a culture of trust

Conversely, being over-sceptical or untrusting with staff or partners creates a negative culture and a climate where people feel they are not valued. This is likely to make them less committed to their work, increase staff turnover and reduce the quality of the work they produce. It has been proved that creating a culture of trust allows staff to become more creative and innovative. They are more willing to express new ideas and to develop and run the business. This positive culture really shows when they deal with customers. It also creates an environment where people feel more comfortable taking risks and making bigger decisions, and will be considerably more committed to solving challenges and hardships. Happy staff that are trusted usually feel empowered to make decisions, which often leads to a better customer experience.

Most of the best ideas to improve businesses come from the staff that work in and run them. They are the ones who see most of the opportunities and issues and understand the customers best in terms of the front line. In many cases, they are closer to the action than you and so they should know more than you. Why not trust them and treat them as you would want to be treated? When staff are treated well, they automatically want to give more and will provide the best insights to create better businesses.

These beliefs and strategies have all come from decades of running a business and making plenty of mistakes along the way. You may be naturally inclined this way, and that will serve you well. But the downside is that you may be more open and vulnerable. If, like me, you are inherently more careful, then you need to learn to trust and let go a little more. A healthy balance of trust-but-verify is ideal.

An example of the benefits of keeping staff feeling positive and empowered happened a few years ago. Rob and I decided to ask all our staff to complete a systems document. We imposed a hard deadline to get it done. We were inspired by our mentorship with James Caan from *Dragons' Den* and presumed that the team would see how it would be a great thing. It was to be a document of all the tasks that each member of staff completed on a daily basis. The idea was that, if they weren't in the office, through sickness or holiday, someone else could read the document and continue in their absence. Business (un)common sense, right?

Well, it was obvious from the behaviour of some of the staff that they weren't focusing on this task very diligently and many of them were clearly reluctant to complete their systems document. Polite reminders fell on deaf ears and tempers started to rise. People stomped around, not making eye contact with management, something that was very far from characteristic of the usually banter-ridden office. It continued as D-day for the systems deadline approached.

When the day came, one person still hadn't completed the task. I was feeling rather combative, so I spoke to our solicitor to get advice and decided to invite this person to a 'performance management meeting'. We'd never done one of these; our previous HR meetings were typically shouted across the office. Clearly, this put her in a defensive frame of mind and the conversation quickly became confrontational. 'You were told when it was due!' we barked. 'That's rubbish, you're just a pair of...' – and before we knew it she had left in a huff and we had a letter from her solicitor.

This solicitor accused us of not managing her job role, stating that we should have considered a medical condition she had. Most of the accusations were intended to boost the possible value of a claim, and this was genuinely the first we'd heard of her needing us to modify her workplace to allow for her condition. However, the reality was that, while we had given her the information and the deadline, I should still have bitten my tongue, been more understanding, listened to her and the team, handled the situation more elegantly and not retaliated. We had lost a good member of staff and the goodwill of the team and we now had a potential employment tribunal looming, with time and legal costs.

Even if you have right on your side, you will end up with a much better outcome if you set emotions aside, talk about solutions, listen, don't react or go on the defensive, and care. It will cost you a lot less time, money and distress and help you avoid difficult issues.

10

Uncommon sense 'gut feeling'

Gut feeling, or intuition, is one of the core decision-making tools
that a businessperson will use. That sense you have inside when looking at a business, an investment or a person is a guiding principle that
you ignore at your peril. Gut feeling is effectively a split-second bio-
logical distillation of an investor's or businessperson's years of experience. It's a sense that can only be acquired through exposure to lots
of good and bad opportunities. This gut feeling guide can be surpris-
ingly accurate for those who are experienced. Obviously, for a person
who has less business or investing experience, this gauge is to be con-
sulted but not relied upon. While your gut feeling is being developed,
rely on diligence, research and analysis to guide your decisions.

I like to run the numbers on an investment, do the diligence and
then sleep on the decision. Usually, my gut, combined with conclu-
sions that my research has drawn, helps me to arrive at a good decision. I never make decisions when emotions are raw. They get in the
way and cloud your vision. In tense moments, it is wise to take some
time to allow the emotional part of your mind to settle and wait for
some objectivity to appear. I guess you could summarize this process
as trust your gut, get proof and verification, then consult your gut
again to make the final decision.

Do not use your intuition if you have no experience in the field;
you may be a good judge of character but you may not yet be a good
judge of the model, class or strategy. It pays to find out as much as
possible first about different classes of business:

- **Old-school commoditized businesses** are well understood:
  knee-deep in competition, they end up having to compete
  on price because they can't differentiate their products
  sufficiently. They are not a place I like to be. Perhaps attractive

from a stability or time-proven standpoint, these types of
businesses usually end up in a race to the bottom on price.
This inevitably leads to low margins and little opportunity to
grow profitability except by increasing volumes.

- **New-world businesses** utilize social media, have a market-
  disrupting element, utilize technology and generally have
  lower overheads. They are preferable to old-school businesses.
- **Information businesses,** which have low or no stock and
  few fixed costs, usually make the biggest margins.

Over time, businesses that stay the same usually experience more
competition as others spot the profit and offer a similar product for
less. It's obvious that you need to pivot and change your product mix
when it gets to the point that you have become a busy fool and a
business is not supplying the returns that allow you to feel your time
is being well spent. Once your business is near to becoming a charity,
it is time to pivot.

Once profits have been made from businesses such as these, it
pays to invest your money in staid, diversified businesses or assets
with lower and often more secure returns. Well-spread capital across
passive income streams such as from property, utility, tobacco, oil or
large consumer product conglomerates such as Unilever, coupled
with some bonds, can reduce volatility and increase the security of
your capital and the income streams that derive from it.

In my teens in the late 1990s, I had a friend who used to rent out
rooms in his house as a way of paying the mortgage. As Sam was
only 18, it was a great route to owning a house and all the benefits that can bring, without having to pay a mortgage. The tenants renting the rooms were not only paying the mortgage but
giving him an income above the mortgage payment. Meanwhile,
the property was sharply going up in value. Of course, managing tenants can be challenging, especially when they are living
with you and have easy access to your time. Not a particularly
conventional character, my friend Sam had some special ways to
ensure that rent got paid and the house was kept in good order.

One afternoon, after becoming increasingly annoyed that his favourite beer was constantly going missing from the fridge, he told me that he had a gut feeling about which of his tenants was stealing it. Visiting him a few days later, I noticed he had a grin on his face and seemed busy with something. As I went over to see what it was, he looked up and said, 'That idiot won't be messing with my beer any more!' I noticed a bright-red bottle labelled 'turbo laxative' in his hand. Proceeding to add the solution to his favourite bottle of beer, he carefully dosed the amber nectar, replaced the cap on the beer and put it back in the fridge. Trap set, later on the evening we sat in the living room watching TV with the tenants when one of them jumped up and rushed to the toilet and slammed the door. We struggled to hold in our laughter when he shuffled back half an hour later. Obviously, he had earlier drunk the 'modified' bottle and was now enduring the consequences. In this way, Sam was able to accurately verify who the culprit was.

Not long afterwards, Sam let everyone know what he had done and said he would do it again periodically to ensure secure storage of his favourite beer. He explained that there was no risk of being 'turbo laxed' if everyone simply ate and drank their own food and drinks. His beer never went missing again. I don't condone his action but it is a good example of putting a problem on its head and finding a (rather harsh) verification solution.

II

Media hype

It is important to understand that the media have their own motives for printing and publicizing news. While I have no problem with that, you should know what those motives are so you can get a balanced view. Most media are capitalist, commercial enterprises run for profit. They are a business and selling is their first and only priority. They will happily make a big claim that is not fully researched or substantiated. This is often done at the expense of the truth, the reality or a balanced view. Be aware of what you read and careful about what you believe. Understand that there are always opposing sides to any argument that may have validity, too.

Later in the book, I will detail the specific publications and resources I prefer and those to steer clear of, so you can gain a balanced view, too.

In almost all cases, headlines are sensationalized, oversimplified and designed as click or wallet bait. They do not have to be true, and there are ways of using the English language to create hype, ambiguity and intrigue to pull you in. The uncommon sense business owner and investor who profits by going against the tide does not base their decisions or knowledge accrual on headlines. Of course, these oversimplified statements have their place because we need information chunked down to reduce overwhelm, but don't hold them in high regard or expect them to tell the whole story. Don't even expect them to be true.

The reality is that life just isn't that exciting or extreme or sensational. Things are usually just a lot more average and uninteresting so, without exaggeration, most publications would not be able to get people to read their newspapers. Unless I'm looking for entertainment (and sometimes I am), I usually focus on publications that are less prone to using these tactics (though they all use them sometimes).

Higher-quality publications that rely less on exaggeration are much more useful because they rely more on hard facts and the quality of their articles.

Media hype to look out for

With regard to business, finance and investing, most of the perennially commented-upon media hype relates to polarized political issues. A popular one is the evil capitalist versus the victim benefits recipient or tenant. I should state my bias up front: I think capitalism is an effective system. I feel this is proven by the fact that all but five nations of the world are built on a capitalist societal system. It is one that has endured centuries and seems mostly fair (in the developed world), or as fair as any single system could hope to be. It generally creates fair competition, and as long as it is well regulated, it seems to reward and encourage enterprise and contribution. That said, I feel the media sensationalizes, stirs up or creates unfounded rhetoric about certain things:

'Higher business taxes would solve many social issues'

Private sector businesses provide most economic activity in the UK today. The private sector effectively funds the public sector. Clearly, many politicians and sections of the population would like businesses to pay more tax. History has shown that creating a larger public sector, which is used to spend this extra tax, is not efficient. The reality is that, usually, this money doesn't go to the right people and it never creates the incentive that we all require to grow. Despite what many people will try to tell you, wastage and poor allocation of resources are much more prevalent in the public than the private sector.

Burdening business owners with ever more 'innovative' (stealthy) taxes (and they have dreamed up plenty since I have been in business) does not encourage business investment, which is the real driver of economic growth, jobs and prosperity. You only need to look at countries with a lower, flat rate of tax to see that tax is easier to collect, investment is encouraged and, overall, the tax take actually increases with a lower tax rate. It sounds crazy, but it's true. You need only talk to some civil servants to figure out the real reason why they can't get the politicians to do this. It would simply be very unpopular with many, and the politics of envy dominates in the UK.

'Generic statements from non–experts are valid'

Most journalists don't invest in or have direct knowledge of the investments they write about. Unless they are specialists in the subject matter and have been at the coalface dealing with the asset class that they write about (this is rarely the case), their views are often regurgitated. The result is a cocktail of what the market believes in general. This is not as credible or helpful as real investment and business experience. An example that illustrates this was when one major broadsheet proclaimed, at the onset of the credit crunch, that 'Buy to let is dead'. The article was mainly predicated on the fact that more buy-to-let lenders had tightened their criteria. The headline is ridiculous, especially when you consider that around 2.7 million households live in houses in this sector, which at the time of writing is also forecast by the Centre for Economics and Business Research (CEBR) to grow by 40 per cent over the next ten years.

Anyone operating in the buy-to-let sector, anyone who truly knows and understands the market, knows that buy to let doesn't 'die' overnight. People working in this sector saw the headline as comical and sensational, but it had a real effect on the less experienced. Conversely, and fortunately for the uncommon sense investor, headlines like this contributed to one of the biggest property buying opportunities in the last 20 years. Thank you, mass media. Thank you, lemmings. Let's hope buy to let dies more frequently.

'All landlords are evil millionaires'

Another headline that never fails to whip up a sensational frenzy is that all landlords are evil millionaires who don't care about their tenants. Publications need a baddie to blame for the woes of the general readership. For those who can't get on the housing ladder, the landlord fits the bad-guy stereotype and becomes an easy target.

The reality, of course, is never as interesting as that. There are good landlords, bad landlords and many landlords in between. Just like anything and everything, you cannot stick them all in one box.

This attitude arises because many people naively believe that that economics is a zero-sum game. They fail to understand that one person having more does not mean that someone else will have less. This is an easy mindset to fall into. It is also convenient and supports a victim mentality. It is far easier for some to believe that the 'millionaires' have taken some of 'their' money than acknowledge that they have simply earned it from enterprise, adding value and sustained hard work. This old-school pantomime continues to be propagated. What is closer to reality is – to play along with the stereotype – that the 'average' landlord will have bought just one or two buy-to-let properties for their retirement.

'The property market is doomed'

Recently, there have been many headlines which claimed that UK Government tax increases in relation to buy to let will kill the sector, or that landlords are doomed because the Financial Conduct Authority (FCA) and the Bank of England are about to further regulate buy-to-let mortgages. The changing tax code will mean that there will be a market shift; landlords will have to adapt, and those that don't will be adversely affected and the sector may shrink. Realistically, though, it is hardly going to remove the private rented sector in one fell swoop. Nor will the increased regulation of banks: the reality here is that banks often hear early about such changes and conform to new rules before they become mandatory. Indeed, 75 per cent of buy-to-let lenders already comply with the proposed changes.

Many people deride things that they don't fully understand. For example, some financial advisers have been down on property since property entered the investment space in 2005, consistently suggesting that the market is doomed. This idea is based on fear and often comes with advice to buy stocks or gold instead. Clearly, they hope that, if they say this for long enough, they will eventually be right, but this doesn't make them good at forecasting; it merely highlights their lack of understanding of the property market.

Many good Independent Financial Advisers behave in this way. When you speak about property, they explain how illiquid it is or how the returns are always lower than equities over the long run. But why compare one with the other? In a balanced world, all classes can be good and all classes can be bad. Success depends on knowledge, experience, sub-niches, timing and other variables. For many years, I listened to the logic of IFAs and wondered what planet they were on; I could get a 30-per-cent return on capital invested with a property investment, versus funds that rarely do better than high single digits over the long run. With time, it became clear to me that they were talking about property funds rather than direct investment in property. But even with this explained, most don't care to listen. They don't invest this way themselves so they don't understand it. Perhaps the truth is threatening to their perceived expertise, or perhaps the truth is simply inconvenient when they earn their fees from selling funds. I'll let you check your own gut feeling on whether an ulterior motive rings true here.

12

Misconceptions, mistakes and lessons in business

Part of the process of working out viable, profitable business strategies is working out and ticking off what doesn't work. Often, you can deduce what does work through what doesn't. By using both the uncommon sense and contrarian philosophies you can increase your chances of success. In this and the next two chapters, I will include observations I've made on popular misconceptions, but also – to balance the view and experience – I will share some of my own mistakes. As discussed previously, learning from the mistakes of others will make you significantly more successful. Take my most valuable mistakes and learn from them vicariously, so you don't have to make them personally.

For balance and detail, the chapter will also cover what I really believe works – after all, this is a 'how to' book as well as a 'how not to' book.

Common misconceptions in business

1 Provide a service that you want rather than what the market wants

Many start-ups and self-employed people get into business because they love something, or are very good at something. In isolation, this is a mistake. Monetizing a passion is part of the process of testing a business or market. However, when the thing you have a passion for doesn't have a market, it's not a business, but a hobby. Many people think that, because they have a problem or a desire, the rest of the world has it, too. You see this from time to time on *Dragons' Den*. Entrepreneurs enter the 'den' passionate and deeply invested in the solution to a problem that doesn't really exist, or perhaps just doesn't have much market appeal. Do not be blinded by your own passions and desires; instead, sanity-check that a sizeable market has the same pains or attractions to your product or service. Don't invest time and money in creating and selling it, or add further overhead to your business, until you've validated the market.

2 Enter a market because there is little or no competition

The most likely scenario, and not what most people want to hear, is that if there is no competition then there is likely to be no market. That is not to say that there is never anything new, but there have been hundreds of thousands, maybe millions, of businesses in every conceivable niche. The chances that you have discovered the one market that is untapped, and destined to be the next Facebook in your industry, is statistically very low. You are well advised to test first rather than jump in with both feet. If you can't find any competition in a marketplace, you will need to find the reason why, because there will be. Is it because there is not much demand or the business model doesn't work?. If your idea stands the test of your due diligence and your version of minimum viable product (MVP), then scale – but not on a whim.

3 Think you're making money because turnover is high rather than focusing on profit (margin)

Turnover is vanity and profit is sanity, as they say. I'd rather make a 10-per-cent profit on £1 million than a 1-per-cent profit on £10 million (unless I had a valuation/sale strategy). While the top-line figures are the same, you will usually have significantly more overhead on a larger turnover. This leaves you with less room to accommodate increasing costs and market changes.

Not all profit is the same. The lower your margin, the more vulnerable you are to change or disruption. Lower margins give you less flexibility and less of a buffer to withstand surprises and changes. In the constant drive for top-line revenue (turnover), it is easy to lose sight of cost control and produce wastage. If you are not careful, you could end up making no more, even on greater turnover. A focus on turnover mostly just drives sales, but a focus on profit drives lower costs, more efficiency, better and increased pricing models, and more.

I have more of a bottom-line (profit) focus. This helps with efficiency but not so much with scale, as I am often concerned with the wastage that scale brings. I favour steady but consistent growth, where costs can be monitored and controlled, over wild but inconsistent growth, where things can get out of control. I think it is good to have someone in your business with the opposite focus. The person who is top-line focused, as my colleague Rob is, drives growth, scale and market share, and maybe valuation in the future. The person who is bottom-line focused – someone more like me – ensures that the enterprise stays lean and efficient and the margins do not evaporate as turnover increases.

4 Ignore the time, labour and materials that go into a product or service

When people don't charge enough for their products or services, they often omit to 'include' or factor in their time investment (in training to become qualified, their experience and the time investment into the specific product or service). Hard costs are only part of the equation when pricing. Staff time is included in the overhead, as is your time, previously sunk costs or staff that have replaced you to free up your time. You could be scaling up a product and selling volumes of something that doesn't even make any money. It could also be swallowing up valuable resources that could be put into better products that make more money.

5 Think 'just do it' is better than doing nothing

If someone is seriously procrastinating, then there is an argument for JDI ('just do it'). More often than not, though, jumping too quickly into a business or launching specific products or services can be a disaster. At best it wastes time and at worst it can make the company insolvent. It is far better to test small with a raw 'version one' of a product or service to a test-market segment (minimum viable product, or MVP) than to just jump in. Test. Tweak. Improve. Scale. Repeat. Don't jump in with both feet. You need to look at the KPIs and profit and loss after each iteration/version to see if it is financially viable to scale. Scaling can be a big mistake if you are scaling a bad model.

6 Believe new is better

One thing I see all the time that makes me shudder is how frequently people think that the new shiny thing will be the saviour and bearer of all riches. I am not sure whether it is naivety, a lack of ability to stay the course, or a fear of missing out (FOMO) on a new opportunity. This mindset is very common, yet it rarely ever works. In most cases, when you have already done the groundwork, it is a far better strategy to figure out how to make that work. Starting again with something else, even if that other new thing looks better, will cost you time, money and learning opportunities.

It takes time to set up solid foundations and to learn sustainable fundamentals. It takes time to build networks, brand and goodwill, a customer database and trust. Every time you move into a new venture, you revert back to zero – the toughest phase in any business. It's nearly all work for little money at the start, and nearly all money for little work at the (longer) end. Doing nothing outrageously exciting or innovative for a long time is better than doing something new all the time.

7 Think you can do it better than anyone

Every small business owner has to let go in order to grow. What you once did (and when your customer would deal only with you) you eventually need to pass on to your team. People don't let go to grow for fear of losing customers or reputation, for fear of others not doing as good a job as they do, or for fear of customers willing to deal only with the owner of the business. Every business owner can relate to this, it happens to us all, and you are not alone. Thousands of businesses have gone through this growth process and, like everyone else, you will have growing pains along the way. The reality is that not only can others do the jobs that you are juggling well, but if you hire the right specialists they can probably do them better than you.

These people can focus on being a master of one area. This is better than you, the self-employed entrepreneur, doing them all to a good enough standard but never mastering them. There are many books on this subject, including *Life Leverage*, *E-myth* and *Built to Sell*.

8 When times get hard, cut marketing costs

In most cases, when businesses have downsized or, worse, gone bust, marketing is the first spending category that seems to be cut. The problem is that marketing brings in most of your sales, so you are effectively killing the golden goose. You have a one-time, small saving but you dry up all your future revenue. If you ran a shop, then your premises are your business. The products sold in the shop are the sales, but the number of people who walk in the door is your marketing. Without it, you must rely 100 per cent on recommendations or referral sales, which will soon dry up if new sales don't keep coming.

Marketing costs should be seen as an investment, almost as part of the fixed overhead, and you should look to reinvest profits into marketing. You should look to invest your entire marketing budget every period, and grow it sustainably. Always be testing new platforms for growth and innovation and measuring existing ones to minimize wastage. React first and fast to change. If you test, measure and tweak your marketing consistently, you reduce the risk of wastage and build a more predictable, sustainable business.

If this is not your core skillset, then you need to hire great marketers in your business. Most people who start businesses aren't marketers but people passionate about their product or service. But a great product with no customers isn't a business; it is an idea or a dream. If marketing is not your skillset, as it isn't mine, then partner, hire or outsource it to those with proven results.

9 Your staff work for you (and should do as you say)

Your staff do not work for you; they work for themselves. They are not working to earn *you* money; they are working to pay their own costs and live their own lives. Dictatorship is not leadership, and it is not in the manual of twenty-first-century business. Of course, business would be so much easier if people just did what they were asked, but to think they will ever serve you peeled grapes on a platter while fanning you is a delusion.

Staff turnover is one of the highest overheads in running a business. It is almost as bad as idle staff doing as little work as possible. You, your business and the profits of both are reliant on your staff doing a great job. Their motives for doing a great job could be money, recognition, to help people and/or something that is completely personal to them. You should care enough about them to listen to them, help them progress their career through understanding their values, listen to their feedback, and give them a career plan and specific feedback to guide them in their growth. If they know you care about them and they feel secure, they will give you the honest feedback you need to grow and improve your business. This is incredibly valuable information that others won't give or you'd have to pay for.

This is not always an easy way to run your business. It can take time and patience. It can test your ability to control your ego and your emotions. Later in the book, you will find a helpful chapter on the three stages of personal development related to business mastery. If there's one major recurring theme in business, it is that those emotions you haven't yet learned to control will keep getting tested, poked and stoked through business challenges. Much as children (apparently) test their parents to the limit, your business challenges will never go away until you grow through them. Don't wish it were easier; wish you were smarter.

> If you have a service mentality with your staff and team, letting them know that you are there to help them progress their career, your business will benefit significantly. An engaged workforce is your best business asset.

10 Working harder and harder will lead to success

What is the best type of work to build your empire? It goes through stages and, in the beginning, putting in the hours can give you a jump-start. However, do not do this blindly on the assumption that a

97-hour week is better than a 37-hour week. I have seen many people work very hard on the wrong things or work hard on the right things but burn themselves out. They overwork to the point where they eventually lose the plot on a client, supplier, or in public, simply because they were fatigued.

I believe that working intensely – in short, sharp, focused bursts – creates results and longevity. In fact, while writing this book, I have used a strategy of 23 minutes of work with a five-minute break. This is followed by a 15- to 20-minute break after every three rounds. You need to work hard on the right things and eliminate the wrong things. You need to leverage, lead and delegate on many things, all of which require smart decision-making and not hard work. In fact, in order to make good decisions, you need time to breathe and think.

This space gives you the clarity to lead effectively and be creative, even though sometimes that can feel as if you are not working hard enough. There is a lot of basic advice out there that says you just have to outwork everyone else. While that may be more true in an athletic endeavour (but, even then, rest, diet and specific training are encouraged), in business higher-level functions like strategy, planning, choosing your battles, focusing on income-generating activities, rest, and thought time are more important than lower-level hard work.

Mistakes I have made in business

This could be a book in itself, so, for the sake of staying on theme, I'll share the edited versions. There is something to be said for making small, frequent, mistakes, but try to avoid making big ones. I've made my fair share, and thankfully none were critical, and all came with valuable lessons disguised within them. Of course, these lessons are only obvious with hindsight. In my early business years, it was more the fear of making mistakes that held me back from making the big, important decisions that would allow me to grow.

1 Spending too much time on small tasks

As someone who often focuses more on saving money, finance and operations than on sales, I have a tendency to get bogged down in saving money. There are diminishing laws of return, where the time it takes to save a small amount actually ends up costing a lot more. The more I have learned to value my time, the better I've become, but I can still get drawn back in from time to time. I see saving money as a sport, a hobby; it feels good to know I got a lower price, a better deal or saved capital that could have been wasted, and that can be my demise. Sometimes I feel the need to beat the system or get one up on an insurance quote, which leads to me spending more time than my time is worth.

You may not have the same 'ism' (a nice way of calling me a geek), but, if you do, it is important to calculate a specific financial number for your time. Work out how much personal profit you bring in each week and divide it by the number of hours a week you work. If you work 30 hours a week and earn £30,000 a week personally, then your time is worth £1,000 an hour. If you can't save that amount of money, or make it, in that hour, then you should be focusing your time and energy on a higher-revenue activity.

2 Being too scared to bare all and connect

I'm not a comfortable marketer or self-promoter, and would happily sit in the background and let my partners take the lead. While you don't have to become a music celebrity, it is still important to understand how valuable a personal brand is, especially in the world of social media. See your personal brand as an asset that you can build on, and invest time in growing and nurturing it. If people can find you on Google, Amazon, Facebook and other platforms, then you should control the narrative and be strategic about what people find and know about you. You have a story, people are interested in that story, inspired by that story, buy from that story, and so you should share that story. If you control your story, then you have more control over your brand. This allows you to dictate to a larger extent what comes up in the main search engines and platforms and can show the more personal side of yourself here.

I suggest having a personal website, a Wikipedia listing, a book on Amazon with your story inside, a Facebook page, profile and group, a Twitter handle, and a fully updated LinkedIn profile as a minimum standard. You can then develop this further into more listings that come up in Google Search, Instagram, Pinterest, Snapchat and so on, if they are relevant in your business model. With people's diminishing attention span, they are looking to find or reject credibility very quickly, so if you are not instantly searchable and your story isn't shared quickly, you don't exist. And that story has to be real, personal, vulnerable and relatable, not just a list of accolades, awards or bragging rights. That, of course, opens you to judgement and criticism, but people will judge you anyway, so you may as well have control.

3 Saving a penny to miss a pound

Fighting for every last penny can damage your business. In my hunt for extracting maximum value, I have pushed savings so far that it has tainted past business relationships. Cost savings should not be the be-all and end-all, and sometimes it is worth paying a little more or being less of a Rottweiler to preserve good relationships. Suppliers and providers don't want to feel backed into a corner and you don't want them to resent you. Choose your battles and, from time to time, let things go or pay a fair price to get fair value and preserve long-term relationships. I can think of occasions where we have screwed down suppliers and, as a result, received poor-quality work, or paid lower salaries only to get less output. I'm not saying that you should be wasteful, but just remember to measure your savings against your time value. Every pound doesn't always need to be a prisoner.

In the past, I've kept costs low by not hiring the best and not paying the best enough. These two things usually go hand in hand. Cost saving is important, but it's important to make sure it is performed on the right things and in the right areas. I would suggest that good people are not an area to scrimp on. Of course, it is not a good idea to have too many staff, or staff sitting idle, but hiring the best is worth it. The best people, when properly tasked, will add many times the value they cost to your business. It can take a little while to really live this way of thinking because it may seem counter-intuitive (certainly to my cost-saving mentality). When Rob and I started, we were very much of the 'save money on staff' mentality. Now, we hire the very best and reward them well. Every day you don't live this principle will cost you in your business. You lose money by failing to provide the highest-quality service to your customers, by making more mistakes and, subsequently, by reduced profitability.

4 Doing things on my own

Like every small business owner or glorified self-employee, the tendency is to do everything on your own because people will not do it as well as you, they don't care as much as you, or they will cost too much money. This is guaranteed to keep you very small, and probably bitter and twisted. You will begin to resent the world and your customers for how hard you have to work for little reward. Yet it is self-inflicted. As already discussed, you have to let go to grow. There are people out there who have strengths in your areas of weakness and passion in the areas you disdain. Find them, pay them and look after them. Endure the short-term chaos that always comes with growth and scale; it will be worth it. It's also significantly more rewarding to share successes with a team, combat loneliness and have support and camaraderie to sustain you through the harder times.

5 Going into the wrong types of partnerships

I'm an advocate of partnerships and joint ventures, but not the wrong ones. That said, sometimes the only way you learn is to go through them. While the main partnerships I've had have been fruitful and sustainable, there have been some that have come and gone. I've tried to learn from each one. Some, like a wild holiday romance, were good for a while but not destined to last. Others probably should never have started, and some could have been worked out with more time and effort from both sides.

Here are some ongoing lessons from building, maintaining and exiting from some partnerships:

- Be careful and wary of going into partnerships with friends. Only take this route if there is a good reason for entering into business with them, and only if you don't mind losing a friend should it not work out.
- Don't take on too many partnerships at once.
- Get a clear agreement first, then define roles and responsibilities.
- Work on your partnerships continually, not just in them.
- Ensure that you having opposing skillsets but an aligned vision.
- Re-evaluate them every now and again.
- Let your partner do their part and get out of their way.
- Trust them until you have reason not to.
- Look to provide at least 51 per cent of the value.
- Celebrate little and often (and sometimes big).
- Forgive small things, say thank you a lot, and sorry.

It is important to have clear agreements with partners up front. Preventing disagreements will save you considerable time and money, and it will allow you to grow your business without getting caught up in things that will harm your relationship. The best way to do this is to write down what you have agreed on paper and agree to the contents. At the very least, have it on email. Depending on the type of relationship you have with this partner, you may choose to enter into an agreement with them such as a consultancy agreement, a shareholders' agreement or the like. Even if you know, like and trust the person, aren't the detailed type or don't like agreements or creating them, I would still strongly recommend you get some sort of agreement clear and agreed up front, or you will be forever cleaning it up later.

6 Not writing books or providing 'content' (podcasts)

As I am more interested in the operational and functional sides of a business, for many years I didn't understand the power of providing content. Of course, we all know that you get more if you give more but, for me, my natural flow isn't reading reams of information. It can take me four hours to write an article, provided I resist all urges to do any-thing else, like research, getting a haircut or cleaning my shoes – things I have no desire to do at any other time. But some things are worth the time investment. Every piece of content you provide can be an asset, as long as you make it valuable, relevant and evergreen. Every article could be found on Google searches, used in the media, shared and published. Your book could be on Amazon for years or even decades, bringing in a constant flow of sales but also supporting and elevating your brand. Your music could be on iTunes for years, your audio content could be accessible on iTunes, Audible and in physical CD format for people to purchase and share. Your podcasts and videos could have hundreds of thousands of subscribers on YouTube, podcasting apps such as Stitcher Radio and other sites. Rob has been nudging me to launch a podcast for weeks; his podcast 'The Disruptive Entrepreneur' is doing very well. Maybe my own is live now, if you are reading this in 2032!

Of course, as information consumption evolves, there will be new and highly leverageable platforms on which to share your message and build a loyal following. Information has never been easier to capture. All you need is a phone, a cheap microphone and a recording device, and you are instantly shareable and consumable across multi-ple platforms. Whatever your business or niche, creating great content (much of it free) will build a base of excited fans who will be your most die-hard supporters, defend you when you are under attack, refer new customers to you and, of course, buy all your products and services. So look beyond the instant sale and focus on putting out great content that delivers great value and you will have a strong brand and business. I'm off to record that next podcast, honestly I am.

7 Hiring people I like rather than people fit for purpose

I think we all unconsciously hire a version of ourselves. We are attracted to people like us, and people like us, like us. So we all have our own insular way of hiring. I mostly look at the CV, as I think that how people have performed in the past is the most accurate predictor of how they will perform and behave in the future. I want to see real experiences and the things they have done.

It has become popular for people to say 'Hire on attitude as aptitude can be taught', but I find that to be mostly wrong. If someone is not capable of doing the job, it is less likely that they will do the job well or enjoy the role, despite their positive outlook. Of course, I am not necessarily right; this is just my personal leaning. I may miss or overlook some real talent because of this approach but, personally, I see it as less of a gamble. My priority is finding someone with proven consistency (because that is what I like to look for) and longevity. Hiring is expensive and risky; a new hire or a bad one can literally cost tens of thousands in recruitment fees, lost revenue, wasted training, new training, customer dissatisfaction, settling in and more.

That said, you need a variety of roles, people, styles and experiences in your team. You wouldn't have 11 goalkeepers, even if the manager were a past goalkeeper himself. You can't hire everyone who mirrors you. You have to hire for the specific role in question, and so, in fact, you are hiring some people who are completely different from you. You are hiring based on the culture of the business as well as the specific role. It is important to consider how people fit and work within a team structure, and how people work together and respond to one another. You need to be very clear about the type of person you need for the role, have a clear job description (JD) and be able to identify key result areas (KRAs) for the role. For higher-level roles, it is important to have more than one person involved in the recruitment and interviewing process.

8 Not understanding the value of mentors and networks

In my early days, I felt inferior around those more successful or further down the business road than myself. It is quite likely that I didn't court the very best people to have in my network or, if I did so, I did it very tentatively. I now believe it to be success-critical to have an extended network of mentors, peers, specialists and inspiring successes that you have access to and friendships and partnerships with. They say your network is your net worth, and I have certainly found that, as my businesses have grown, so has the quality of the people I have access to. It will, of course, happen naturally over time, but you can accelerate it by investing time consciously and persistently into the area of building your network and courting the most valuable players (MVPs) and A-listers in your industry. According to Tony Robbins, you are the sum of the five people you spend the most time with. So it holds true that you can increase your net worth by investing in and working on your network, and by seeing it as an income-generating asset just like a property or any other asset class.

9 Accepting what those who appear to be in authority tell you

Over the years, I have had various battles with those in authority, especially when I think they are wrong on an issue. Council planning departments frequently tell people to do things or refuse to grant planning consents that are later overruled by the inspector as being incorrect. Courts (especially at the county court level) are frequently overruled by higher courts. Police and parking wardens often have their penalty tickets cancelled as being incorrectly issued, too. The key is not to automatically accept what someone tells you or puts in a letter just because they are in a position of authority. Of course, most of the people I mention above are there to help the system run smoothly and should help your life. However, there can be times when you feel an injustice is happening. In these instances, verify what they are saying by gathering evidence and passing it to an independent, non-conflicted specialist for advice.

Be careful to pick your battles. In the past, I have wasted time on small issues that were not worth the time or negative mental energy. In the long run, it will cost you more in the development of your business and your personal wellbeing. Let most issues go.

As our company Progressive Property has grown over the years, occasionally a situation has boiled up. As much as I don't want it to end that way, it sometimes winds up in a spat. One such scenario started as a small parking issue in the business park we trade from and grew into a major confrontation. As we developed more courses, more delegates came to our site. More delegates mean more cars, which all need parking spaces. A few years ago, we started to write to customers to ask them to park at a car park we have arranged for them close by. But, as with many areas of life and business, some just didn't listen and continued to park where they shouldn't. As we added more small business courses to our training programmes, the parking situation reached breaking point and one of the other residents started to try to whip up support to get us thrown out of our buildings. As he had a quasi-legal staff member in his office, he rounded up the other residents at a site management meeting to tell them what threats he wanted to issue and that he wanted to have us removed (even though we own the freehold).

I went along to the next meeting with solutions jotted out and ready. I soon found that two of the most vocal protagonists had persuaded the chap who runs the management company to say that if we did not stop running training courses from the site they would take us to court for breeching covenants we entered into when we bought the site. I could have gone away, sold our stake in the buildings and it would have cost us several hundred thousand pounds. However, as we had made a significant investment in the site, I decided we couldn't be bullied and hired a lawyer to provide advice. The advice came back that the covenants supplied by the management company had been changed and were not enforceable or relevant. It was also pointed out that, as the biggest owner on site, we owned 30 per cent of the management company, making any action very difficult without our consent – consent that would be obviously be impossible to obtain as we would be taking action against ourselves.

We made further changes to the way in which we verified who is parking on site and improved signage and seating areas. As I read the information I had received to the committee, they quickly backed down and continued on to the next topic as though many already knew this to be the case. Don't believe everything you are told, especially from those who have a vested interest in telling you something that doesn't benefit you.

Mistakes our competitors make in business

No businessperson is going to fill in a feedback form for their competition of all the mistakes they are making. But competition is healthy: it creates and keeps a fair market and so common mistakes made by competitors set precedents that you can learn from, so they benefit everyone, including you.

1 Instant gratification

Business models that have the draw of making big money very quickly, or that like to create the illusion of this, rarely last long. If it were that big and easy, everyone would be doing it. Many get-rich-quick business schemes either simply do not work or generate their profits at the expense of customers. This might give the impression of working initially, but will usually come back to haunt the architects. The perceived wisdom among some less experienced entrepreneurs that they should focus on the utopia of fast money, earned with little work, is usually folly. In my opinion and experience, slow and silly wins the race and is a much better model for success, due to compounding, momentum, leverage and sustainability.

I have seen some unscrupulous entrepreneurs perform share sales to inexperienced investors in businesses they know to be unprofitable or doomed, for a lump of cash. But at what cost? The investors often don't understand what they're investing in, and they find themselves buying into unrealistic predictions provided by the people selling the businesses. The result is always the same: the inexperienced investors end up losing large amounts of money. As reputation is everything, the operators face the consequences of losing their status and credibility – essentially killing all their future earnings for some quick and easy cash at investors' expense.

2 A focus on competing on price

When you start undercutting your competition, you place yourself on a slippery slope to very thin margins and, therefore, an unsustainable business. This, of course, isn't exclusive to competitors in our business but something found in every industry. People assume that, by charging a low price or one lower than their competitors, they will get more customers. This is a common fallacy. If something looks cheap, many people will be sceptical of the amount of value they can get from it, and low prices often reveal a lack of confidence and experience.

When you charge reduced prices compared to your competition, you also attract the lower end of the customer market. These customers want more for less and often take up more time and overhead in your business. They may also be your most difficult customers to deal with and keep happy. You also, ironically, repel the better customers because they will pay a higher price for a higher level of product or service. We have seen many competitors come into the market and charge day rates that aren't sustainable. They often struggle even to fill their quota, and soon enough they give up and move on to doing something else. It is far better to have lower-volume, higher-margin products and services as you start; you can always negotiate to reduce your price if you are forced to, but it is rare that you will be able to negotiate an increase.

3 Selling too much or not at all

Platform sales are not my flow and, if I had my way, I'd probably never sell in a way that wasn't consultative. The problem with that mentality is that you would probably not make much money, and not a lot moves until someone sells something. You normally witness the extremes when it comes to selling: people like me who aren't overtly selling versus people who are sell far too hard and become pushy.

When you push too hard, everyone avoids you like a bad smell. Sure, you will get a few sales through attrition but, as you scale, it begins to look bad and desperate on your part. Why not be, or hire, a balance between the two extremes: someone who is happy to sell but does it with an elegance that preserves the long-term relationship and prizes reputation over a quick hard sale? It is important to know when to push a little and when to hold off for a future sale. Learn and practise sustainable sales techniques to build relationships rather than cheap closer-gimmicks.

There are multiple ways to practise sustainable selling rather than just direct selling. It is easier than ever to create tribes, communities, followers/followings and fans, at a very low cost and with no real risk. You can grow your reach on all the social media platforms like Facebook, Twitter, YouTube, LinkedIn, Snapchat, Instagram and podcasts. These platforms allow you to communicate, interact and add value to your subscribers, readers and listeners. You can build a mutually beneficial relationship and a network together so that you become a trusted authority. This approach makes selling a more pleasant, smooth and sustainable experience. Don't just ask for money when you need it; strive to continually give value and serve your network. Then, when you do have something to offer, you will have a swarm of hungry buyers ready to buy from you.

4 Lack of patience and long-term thinking

There is a saying that people overestimate what they can achieve in a short time but underestimate what they can achieve in a lifetime. I fully endorse this. I've witnessed so many people and companies who lack the patience to keep going, or make very short-term decisions that affect their future adversely. You can't expect wild success at the start, but if you do get it, you should be extremely grateful. Don't let it distort your vision of yourself, see it as beginner's luck and behave in a way that keeps you open to improving.

We live in an instant-fix society. The media glorifies success in an edited form and there are always a plethora of schemes and scams to test your long-term outlook. It is far better to go slow for a long time than to go wildly fast and burn out. If at first you don't succeed, tweak, pivot, iterate. These are all Silicon Valley terms for improving and trying again. Many people don't see the downside of starting again, only the big promise, hype and excitement. One of the big downsides of the fast and frenzied approach is that you get a reputation for being a stop-start-stop-starter. When you develop a track record like this, few will risk time or money with you in case you are on to something else before they know it.

5 Can't take the heat and the criticism

Business at the big boys' level is not for the faint-hearted. Your vulnerabilities, lack of self-worth and defensive ego will all be put to the test. You put yourself out there and ask the world for money, so you can't expect not to have critics, haters and even trolls (stalkers and critics via anonymous online profiles). Sometimes the criticism isn't fair; sometimes you did your best but made a mistake. Who doesn't make mistakes? I can't say it gets easier or better, but I can say that you can get better at having strategies and experience to neutralize these negative events through good communication, elegant PR, or lawyers if it has to go that far. With regard to legal avenues, tread carefully; often there's only one real winner when lawyers are involved, and it often isn't the claimant or defendant.

Many people take criticism very personally, and you can't blame them, but what they don't realize is that it happens to everyone. The better and more successful you become, the bigger and stronger the criticism grows. In the early days, I naively thought that the better I got, the fewer critics I would have. Thankfully, I am the quieter one in my business partnership, so my partner gets more of it than me, and I'm OK with that.

13

Misconceptions, mistakes and lessons in finance

As in business, part of the process of working out viable, profitable finance strategies is working out and ticking off what doesn't work, using both the uncommon sense and contrarian philosophies to increase the chances of success. As already discussed, learning from the mistakes of others will mean you don't have to make them yourself.

Common misconceptions in finance

1 Buying new is better

Many people assume that something will have a lower maintenance cost if it is new. This is not always true. With new property, you get snags and newer isn't always cheaper on an ongoing basis. In almost anything you buy new, especially cars and houses, there will be significant depreciation from new. People love the thought of owning new for emotional reasons, but in finance and investing second hand is where the depreciation curve significantly levels off, will cost you less and is likely to appreciate more. In some instances, such as certain car marques, financing new can be cheaper for the period of ownership, so never assume and always work out the true cost of purchase and ownership.

Some of my favourite examples are things like offices and phone systems. Buying a new office (or house) will usually be an inferior investment compared to buying one that is a few years old. A little like new houses, offices will usually depreciate, at least for the first few years of their lifespan. For example, at the time of writing an office in Peterborough, my home city, might be £130/ft to buy as a ten-year-old existing unit, half the cost of having it built as a new unit. The reality is that, in ten years, the value of the new and used one will probably have come together and both may be worth, say, £150/ft. All other things being equal, the older office would prove to be £120/ft better as an investment. £120/ft over 3,500 sq. ft (enough space to house, say, 30 staff) works out to £20,000. This leaves a lot of cash to pay for works to get the building right for the occupant, like cabling, lighting, office fit-out, and some spare change to reinvest or capital to stash and look at with joy.

A common item that companies will try to sell new to entrepreneurs is expensive phone systems costing many thousands of pounds. Of course, they are a necessity (according to the salesperson), a little like the new server that the IT maintenance company tells you is a must-have every few years. I would take time to consider whether you actually need such items for your business. It's often better to start on a shoestring and buy these items later, when you scale and you really do need them. Some may sell you on the ability to 'grow into' a phone, computer or IT system, whereas I have a philosophy of 'grow out'. Capital should be closely guarded within start-ups, and every pound treated like a prisoner you don't release easily. Other examples are office furniture, which seems to have huge mark-up and huge depreciation. Why not go to a liquidation sale or search on eBay for the items you need? Let someone else suffer the depreciation for you. And you don't need the best computers with the fastest chips and fancy gadgets; buy middle of the range or equipment that is fit for purpose, not for showing off.

2 Owning (or renting/leasing) is better

In much the same mentality that says buying new is better, the old-fashioned thought process is to buy something only when you can afford it, and never use credit/debit to buy anything. Mostly, I agree that credit is not good for depreciative assets, but the true cost of both finance and ownership should be calculated and the total true cost of 'ownership', including fees, purchase and exit costs, and also factors of convenience, should all be accounted for. It is currently significantly cheaper in a two- or three-year ownership period to contract-hire a new Mercedes, Audi or BMW from an Internet broker than it is to buy new, or even two or three years old. Plus, you don't have to deal with the hassles of buying and selling from private sellers. Sometimes it is best to take an option to purchase a property, or a rent-to-rent, than it is to buy it. Sometimes it is best to lease an office rather than buy it. Of course, sometimes ownership is better too, but only if you are well capitalized, you know you are settled, the cost of finance is relatively low and you're in the right part of the cycle.

3 Saving money is good

Saving money is actually only one level up from spending money. When rates are low and inflation outstrips interest, then saving money can be less profitable. Having savings in cash can be costly and having more than you need to protect you against the downside and self-insure might not be a profitable way forward.

There are two caveats here. You should not invest if:

- you are new to investing and you have no savings – build a savings fortress first
- rates are high and you get a good return on savings that outperforms or equals other investments and beats inflation. This, however, is not likely to happen for a long time to come.

These two factors aside, you should ring-fence capital away from the banks by investing at first in low-risk regulated investments. Then, as you build layers of wealth, you can increase your investments into more speculative or higher-risk vehicles. You will then need to diversify and insure your wealth, and you won't be doing that by putting it back in the bank.

4 It's OK to change and start again

I have written a chapter dedicated to this anti-phenomenon because I see it so often and it erodes wealth on such a vast scale. With finance, you have fees attached, opportunity cost in terms of time, and front-loaded costs where more interest than repayment is loaded at the start of your loan duration. Because of these factors, you do not want to chop and change your finance unless you get a significantly better deal that is calculated through the lifetime of the loan. The cost of change is often hidden and ethereal. When you are able to analyse this in business, finance and investing, you will profit by going against the tide.

5 All IFAs/financial advisers know what they are talking about

Of course, not all IFAs/financial advisers are the same. The point here is always to verify and research anyone giving financial advice; after all, it is your money at stake. Many do not invest in what they advise, and get greater commissions for advising certain products. Some are new recruits in high-street banks, keyboard warriors on forums or social groups with no real experience. You will care about your wealth more than anyone else, and one of the single best investments of your time is to learn about money and finance and how to deploy, manage and grow it effectively. Sure, we all want to leverage and outsource, but you wouldn't outsource the birth of your child or their upbringing (with the exception of maybe a part-time nanny), so don't outsource the management and responsibility of your finances.

6 Raising finance is always good

Raising finance has associated risks that should not be ignored because you need the money. The more you need the money, the more desperate you will seem/be, and the more you will give away in equity or cost of finance. Large loans can add strain to the cash flow of a business, high rates can turn an otherwise profitable invest-ment upside down, and selling equity in your business can give away control. Large lumps of cash, though enticing to think about, often cause people to become irrational and make silly decisions. Lottery winners are a good example of this. Of course, raising finance cre-ates leverage, but you should not look for more money until you can effectively manage what you already have.

Mistakes I have made in finance

1 Not measuring financial metrics enough

One of the most important things to do in finance is to measure everything: net worth, profit and loss, balance sheet, business overhead, all costs, direct debits, personal spending ... everything. You cannot master what you do not measure. In my early entrepreneurial ventures, I did not measure all this useful data, and so I was at a disadvantage for making good strategic decisions. Never again will I make this most fundamental of errors, especially when it is so easy to correct. It is also fun to measure all your financial KPIs, especially if you are a bit obsessively self-controlled like me, and you get a real-time, accurate measure of your progress. When it moves forwards and upwards, that feels good and you see, in hard numbers, the fruits of your labour and passion.

As your income from assets and business increases, it becomes easier to cover your day-to-day expenses and reinvest income to create a bigger income. When you increase your lifestyle commensurately each time your income increases, you become a slave to your income. Why not set some big targets as to how much of you will save each month for further investment?

With time, the power of compounding becomes immense and unstoppable. Like a giant snowball that gets bigger and bigger with each turn, the returns you make on returns you saved from last year get reinvested. They make further returns and so on, meaning you gain exponential increases in wealth. I set myself a target to spend less than 25 per cent of my income, without fail. This leaves plenty of cash spare for further investment, and so the snowball gets exponentially bigger. I have found that a focus on this compounds it further, because preserving and utilizing capital creates more income, which creates more capital, which creates more income. Soon enough, you will struggle to spend 25 per cent of your total earnings per period, no matter how hard you try or how frivolous you become.

2 Relying on my own capital and not enough leverage

In my investing and business ventures during my teens and early twenties, I moved from venture to venture and saved most of the capital profit I made. I had Internet businesses before they were popularized by sites like Amazon and eBay. I would bring in cars from overseas and sell them in the UK. My dad instilled in me the core principle of 'spend nothing and save everything', but he took it to extremes. Because of this, I formed the very old-fashioned view that you should never invest money you don't have, and save hard. Part of that strategy saves wasted capital, but it doesn't harness the power and benefits of leverage and therefore slows progress significantly.

In my opinion, you need to balance leverage. Without enough leverage, it is only your capital, and not other people's, that is working for you. If you over-leverage then you expose yourself to risk and small changes in the market, and the costs of the capital will outweigh the income. I leaned too far on the side of overcautious and under-leveraged, while many people were at the opposite end of the spectrum. While this approach protected me, it also slowed me down.

3 Borrowing money at a fixed rate or with fees

Thankfully, if I have ever borrowed money, I have always paid it back with a return. I am far too concerned with losing someone else's money to take undue risks. However, in lending and borrowing fair sums for hundreds of properties and other assets and overheads, I've learned from the relatively harmless, though often naive, mistakes I have made in my journey.

In the past, I have taken too many fixed-rate mortgage products out as a hedge against rising interest rates. While it might be a good idea to have some debt fixed, overreliance on these products usually ends up costing you more. A little like an insurance product, fixed rates usually have already factored into their interest rate what the market believes will happen to interest rates over the period of the product. On top of this, there is likely to be a margin for taking the product out, a little like an insurance premium. Clearly, you can only make a decision on whether a fixed rate offers good value or not when you compare it with what tracker rates are available and, more importantly, the period over which the mortgage is to be taken. Combined with the initial product fee and an exit fee, these are the most important factors to consider. I usually opt for a tracker; I take the difference between the fixed and the tracker and put this in an account as my own insurance buffer to cash flow the mortgages, should rates rise for a period. In my early years, I didn't realize just how much these fees add up and dramatically increase the actual rate you pay.

I have nearly taken out complicated foreign currency mortgages, which have lower rates, or those traded against other currencies, in a bid to reduce the value of my loan over time. I have found that most of these schemes end up working for a while, but the risk of the currency you have borrowed appreciating and your repayments and mortgage balance against sterling going up are very real. I find that the simpler I can keep any transaction, business or investments, the better. And these types of products are the opposite.

In the past, I have also borrowed money from commercial and bridging lenders who are heavy on 'other' fees. These can include arrangement fees, fees for solicitors who are instructed by the lender (on top of your usual conveyancer), fees for valuations during a project, and exit fees (which can even be linked to the gross development value of a project). As stated, and to be assumed for any type of loan, it is important to include all of these fees in your appraisal to get an 'all-in' rate. I can, for example, think of one development funder who says they charge around 7-per-cent interest, but in reality this works out to an 'all-in' rate of more like 12 per cent plus. You usually won't get bridging finance lower than an 'all-in' rate of 15 per cent once you add on all the fees. This is fine if it's the only way you can get the money and there is enough profit in the deal, but often there isn't and you can become a busy fool, with less money than you started with. Personally, I would prefer to do a smaller project, use cheaper finance or my own funds, and make the same amount of money with less time and risk.

Mistakes our competitors make in finance

1 Not working on meeting and building relationships with banks

Borrowing money used to be about getting dressed up and meeting your bank manager. If you could make him or her your family friend, it boosted your credibility and helped in securing loans. In recent years, lending has become more automated and the computer decides 'Yes' or, often, 'No'. As you move up the food chain from residential to buy to let to commercial lending, it again becomes important to build and nurture a relationship with your bank manager. Many local competitors rely on brokers who end up getting them less flexible deals, higher rates and a higher risk of a decline. Relationships with good banks and the good people within them will make a difference to your ability to borrow and will be an investment of time that will pay you handsomely. It can be very tempting to jump from bank to bank or be lured in by the marketing of the challenger banks and their competitive terms. Do not have a fling and ruin the marriage.

2 Spending and borrowing emotionally rather than logically

I will talk about the main emotions that drive bad investing and business decisions at the end of this chapter. These core lessons also carry over into finance. If you borrow money when you are desperate for it, and fear or greed are driving the borrowing decision, you will likely take unnecessary risks just to get the money. You will be too quick to offer too much security, and you will end up paying exorbitant fees and unsustainable interest rates. Be very careful not to spend or borrow money when your emotions are heightened. Sleep on it. Think about it. Search out more viable alternatives that don't give so much away. In many cases where money has been loaned or borrowed and lost, desperation or greed were driving the deal, which then ended up being one-sided and unsustainable.

3 Spending, investing and borrowing in the wrong areas

This can be in the form of over-the-top expensive offices and cars creating the illusion that an enterprise has more wealth than it does, or that it is a bigger competitor than it is. It can also involve raising debt for everything from computer equipment, furniture and cars, to things not seen by the public and other depreciables. While preserving capital is something I thoroughly advocate, I would also consider raising finance rather than spending cash if the absolute cost of ownership were lower. However, these aren't the reasons I have seen competitors adopt this strategy. They are often on a vanity offensive and, before they know it, they have put a huge pressure on their overhead.

4 Not getting charges/security

There have been some relatively low-profile cases in the property space where people with apparently good reputations have borrowed money from clients, and then things have gone wrong in the form of late repayments, court cases to force repayments, and sometimes reputational damage. There is nothing wrong with borrowing money, but I believe it should be done carefully and with diligence by ensuring that proper security is given/received in the form of a charge, or at the very least a restriction. In addition, a fair interest rate should be agreed (too high and the borrower will struggle to pay it back, too low and the lender won't earn fair interest) and a proper contract or loan agreement should be drawn up with clear terms, time frames, and 'what ifs' for if and when things change or go wrong. Do not get emotional about, or rush into, borrowing or lending money. Follow the proper course of action and the necessary steps for protection.

5 Using interest-only or repayment mortgages/loans

When it comes to borrowing on interest-only or repayment terms, most people seem to go to either extreme. Of course, you have to pay back loans, but loan repayments against some asset classes actually increase the monthly payment, which in turn reduces cash flow. In fact, you can't get a repayment mortgage from many buy-to-let lenders as the rental coverage calculation will not be met; this is a KPI that informs the lender of the cash-flow viability of a loan.

To use a specific example, in order to make a property cash flow, where growth has hundreds of years of proven data, getting an interest-only mortgage will increase the monthly cash flow. In this case, as long as you make sensible provisions, inflation/house price growth should largely cover the capital repayment at the end of the term, with significant equity remaining, and the cash flow collected for the term.

Conversely, in some cases, repayment loans are a better choice. If there is enough margin in the monthly income, having a repayment mortgage will reduce the capital sum over time, negating the hit of a full capital lump in the future. It is nice to see your equity go up in two ways: market growth and loan reduction. In addition, many commercial lenders will not give interest-only loans, so the choice simply isn't there. If you factor the monthly repayment cost into your figures, it may force you to find a better deal to cover the increased costs of finance. Ultimately, anything that creates better deals is a good thing, as long as it remains possible to acquire the deals. Lastly, repayment mortgages will often have lower interest rates, so it is sometimes better to go for a repayment loan at, say, 3 per cent over the equivalent interest-only loan at, say, 5 per cent.

14
Misconceptions, mistakes and lessons in investing

As an investor, it is usually better to buy good assets that are poorly marketed. A good example of this is finding a house for sale with an old-school estate agency that doesn't have a great marketing presence. These agencies often have a bad location, poor online presence, poor branding and lack of proactive sales staff, all of which are usually a sign that it is the perfect location to find a deal. If the property itself is in poor condition and you can add value with refurbishments to make it worth a lot more, even better. Commercial buildings are the same, as are many consumer products. Costco is another good example as they offer really good high-quality products at low prices. Their marketing activity is minimal and relies on a membership-based customer base; their products are often higher in quality than some of the big brand names on the high street.

Unloved assets in any part of the economic cycle can prove to be a great thing. As we know that the value of assets is partly linked to the expectation of their value in the future, it is good to invest in ones which the market sees as boring or unlikely to be a good thing in the future, if you believe the opposite to be true. Commodities, property, precious metals, wine, cars, watches have all been in or out of favour in each cycle; your job is to decipher which one has fallen or risen too far.

Common misconceptions in investing

1 You can time the market

This misconception is rife. You hear considerable street talk about it, but it is virtually impossible without hindsight. It is a fool's game to short-term trade trying to time the market, and there have been a plethora of cases with investors losing their shirts trying to do this. Warren Buffett has stated that you can predict what will happen in the market, but not when. If you could time accurately what will happen and exactly when it will happen, you could be a billionaire very quickly. Of course, many investors or traders have apparently timed the market perfectly. Having had many candid and close discussions with investors and business owners who have made millions from 'good timing', they have all stated to me that the timing felt right but had an element of luck about it, too. They were able to fall back on their decades of experience to get a gut feeling and make a decision, and then the element of luck that no one can predict or reverse-engineer played its part. Every person I speak to, in the cold light of day when egos are dropped (and maybe wine is flowing), also has stories of situations and decisions where they did something similar but the result was worse.

Never risk a significant percentage of your wealth on a timing-based business, investing and finance decision. Understand that, if you are making decisions in this manner, there is a large element of speculation in your actions.

2 Hotspots make more money

Littered throughout this book are stories of hotspot chasing that mostly end in failure. If you even and average out over long periods of time (at least one cycle of 15 years or more), you see that the effect of fast growth in some 'hotspot' areas eventually levels out. In the UK property market, for example, you might see growth averaged out and backwards over a cycle of 7 per cent a year, year on year. Remember that a hotspot usually isn't one in reality, only in hype. But let's humour this idea for a moment and assume that the marketed hotspot was, in fact, hot. It will likely be a hotspot for a short part of the cycle, as when the Olympics came or when there is regeneration or actual rail links created, but this will not be sustained through the cycle. In other parts of the cycle, the growth will be lower by comparison to compensate, and when evened and averaged out through the cycle, it will be roughly in line with the national average, give or take decimals of a per cent. The part that many fail to add to the equation and factor in is the increased cost, time and lack of control caused by chasing hotspots (which will fall out of your area of expertise and geography unless you are very lucky). Even 30 to 50 miles will increase time and cost enough to erode a percentage or two, which can be your entire net margin.

The more you get to know a concentrated area (geography, class, niche), the better the returns, the lower the costs of management, maintenance, mistakes and more. Hotspot chasing is emotional and impulsive, not a well-researched and holistic decision that takes in all the factors and costs.

3 Saying 'Let's negotiate' is a good tactic

If you are ever in a negotiation, don't tell the other party that's what you are doing. The second you say, 'Let's negotiate', or anything about being in a negotiation, you have revealed too much. Smart people will know you are ripe for an easy picking; other people may feel manipulated. You frequently see this naivety on shows like *The Apprentice* and *Dragons' Den*. Another important point on negotiation is not to negotiate too hard. Sure, if you are entering a one-time, never-to-be-repeated deal when you will never see the vendor again, you may make some silly offers. However, in most cases, you will simply irritate the vendor and damage your reputation. That damage will affect you much more quickly than the years it took to build a good one.

> A lie gets halfway around the world before the truth has a chance to get its pants on
>
> *Winston Churchill*

4 It's all about the return

Many people love to invest based on the percentage income return they will receive from an investment. This is especially true when it comes to overseas investors or out-of-area investors. I have seen many examples of buildings sold on a yield (return) basis as the be-all and end-all. One such example was a building that sold in Peterborough to a group of investors from the Far East. The sale was made solely on the basis that it would return X-per-cent income. The building was sold for around 35 per cent more than was considered a fair price by the local developers I spoke to, and that even left some profit for the developer. Following further enquiries with the purchasers, it became apparent that the they were 'happy as long as they get a 6-per-cent return'.

The reality is that, once a development is complete, its value will be around 20 per cent less than the total cost of purchase and development. This destruction of capital means that the real return is negative for the first few years, as income is needed to make up the capital losses that would be incurred were the building to be sold. I doubt the investors really understood this, and I doubt they would have made the investment if they had. Many high-net-worth Middle Eastern, Chinese and Russian investors dumping money into the UK may not care much but, even if I had half the world's wealth (and my business partner the other half), I think I would.

Investing mistakes I have made

Many of my mistakes have been exposed in this chapter already and are relevant to this section, or laced through the rest of the book. They include getting sucked into buying investments that were new, overpriced (because they were new), overseas or too far away from me to be able to manage them effectively, chasing deals and pushing the price up, waiting too long, being too tight and wanting to pay too little, and more. I am sure you are enjoying my pain, so I may as well lay it all out and detail some more that we haven't already covered.

1 Too management-intensive

If an investment is too far away or you need to be too involved in its management and it becomes too much to manage, this can add to its 'true cost'. It is therefore important to add into your analysis and decision making the time and costs needed to manage an asset, class or business. However, most people miss these because they are hidden, not marketed by sellers and you often only know the true costs after six months to a year. Be sure to factor in the cost of travel, cost of ownership, fees, cost of entry and exit, depreciation, staffing and, very importantly, your time invested, when entering into anything related to business, finance or investing. This is the only way to find out the true cost of an asset. Unfortunately, most people just look at the purchase price and value.

2 Chasing deals too hard

I have experienced many dichotomies in investing. How much do I chase a deal? Do I wait and let it come back to me while I meditate barefoot? It is a constant balancing act that may rarely be in true equilibrium, but you will build intuition as you gain more experience. You want to be keen but not needy, willing to commit but also willing to walk away. At times, you will really want or need to close deals like the ones we got in mid-2016, where we had significant excess capital burning a hole and wanted/needed some buildings to invest into. Fortunately, some of the sold prices were so high that, even if I had been desperate, I would still not have gone anywhere near them. During this period, I tried to be self-aware enough to know when I am more vulnerable to paying too much money and chasing too much.

3 Waiting too long/being too tight

This is the inverse of the above: I have been known to wait too long and, be too tight and, as a result, I have lost some deals that looking back would have been great. I could have bought them with a small increase. This hindsight is as unhelpful as it is useful because you have to set a maximum price and you never know how far someone else will bid up. If you are more left-brain then, like me, you may find yourself with this same challenge. It seems that most people have the previous problem of chasing deals too hard or desperately.

Investing mistakes our competitors make

1 Incorrect levels of leverage

Leverage is a fine balance. Too much and you increase risk and exposure to small changes in finance and markets. Too little and you are not getting the benefit of extra (other people's) capital. You need a buffer for corrections that take into account significant drops and sale costs. It is not for me to tell you your level of leverage, or loan to value across your portfolio of businesses, assets and classes, as that is for you to calculate. It will also change as your attitude to risk changes, your wealth grows and the market runs through the cycles. Some may want 50 per cent loan, 50 per cent equity. Others may want 60 per cent. I would suggest that much more than 70 per cent on initial purchase (that then settles at 60 per cent with growth and repayment) is risky. I would suggest that going lower than between 40 and 50 per cent may be under-utilizing available capital resources, especially if lending and rates are low.

2 Too operational

If you remain hands on once you have built an income stream or business model, you will limit your growth. In order to grow, you must let go. It is tempting to keep your hand in or, worse, stick your beak into the operations of every part of your business or portfolio. This can waste hours every day, cause paranoia, over-controlling thoughts and actions, and disable your ability to switch off. It is, therefore, unsustainable. No one likes being monitored and micromanaged either. It is like the landlord who stays stuck in the details of tenancy agreements, collecting rent, doing the maintenance, instead of outsourcing those parts to professionals and focusing on being an investor who does deals and puts teams together.

3 Too short term

Most investors invest based on what is likely to happen this week, this month or at best next year. If you extend that to a 10-, 20- or

30-year view, it changes the game. You are able to be more patient, more strategic, more focused, more committed and, overall, you make better decisions. Of course, in our world of instant gratification, this isn't easy for most people; schemes play on our emotions and desires for the easy short cut. It starts with creating a vision, knowing your purpose and then making a plan. Keep going towards your vision and tweak the plan as you go, but do not let everything that falls in your lap distract you from your purpose. These flighty opportunities will be here today and gone tomorrow, but you will be with yourself for ever.

4 Investing in what's in vogue, what's hot and what others tell them is good

As we have said, and will continue to say, the uncommon sense philosophy is the opposite of this. You mostly profit by going against the tide, not with it. Refer back to Chapter 5, 'Priced in' and 'real value', if you need a reminder of this.

5 Buying assets that look good/shiny and make good social chat

Nice holiday houses, cars, new office buildings, popular stocks; these all look good and sound good when we talk about them. Which means they are most likely the opposite. In fact, 'Where there is muck there is money' is often true. You want to find assets that are away from public view, assets that have inherent value through disrepair, the wrong function, not currently functioning, or latent potential that is not yet found.

To me, it was 'common' sense not to buy a Ferrari: big maintenance, high outlay, poor utility and eye-watering depreciation on new models. After much persuasion, I accepted that perhaps it might be uncommon sense and Rob and I purchased what I called at the time the 'indefensible' Ferrari 430 Spider. We kept it for five years and only lost £6,500 (yes, really). Rob thinks it was because we bought the 'worst 430 in the UK', but I stick to my guns that we bought it at the right time. By 2015 I had mellowed to the idea of replacing it. As much as it went wrong, didn't go round corners properly, rusted, needed a new clutch every 5,000 miles and leaked water, it still looked and sounded pretty good. After a three-month, Rob-style, daily campaign listing all the benefits of replacement for the newer, outrageously priced Ferrari 458 Spider, I finally relented and we made the purchase. A world away from the old car, this new one really was amazing. Gearbox issues had been sorted with the double clutch system, it felt and sounded much better and went round corners as if on rails – or so I thought.

After a few days of driving it, hood down and the Manitou switch set to 'race' so the exhaust baffles would open and make it louder, I was in love. Finally, the dream of owning a Ferrari had become reality – until early one morning, when my phone rang. At that time of the morning it would usually mean Rob with bad news. 'I've crashed the Ferrari. It's gone through a hedge; the brakes wouldn't work but I don't think there's that much damage.' I drove to work to find our £168 k, one-week-old purchase sitting in a heap at the side of the road, a full 30 yards from the 'hedge'. The car took six months and £98 k to repair. The insurer questioned whether they should be taking action against Ferrari for the defective brakes, until the repairer said that the brakes were fine and just needed a lot of warming up. In the end, the insurer paid out and we ended up with a brilliant car that we love. It is probably uncommon sense to have some things which most would say are crazy purchases, as none of us are getting any younger.

Various property models existed mainly prior to the 2007 financial crisis, including the well-documented new-build upmarket apartment projects that were very low yielding and overpriced. Paying significant sums over market value for many sites, these investors ended up with mortgages that cost more every month than the rental income and made huge losses if they chose to sell the properties. Many were forced to keep the properties until the capital growth caught up and the value of the apartments reached levels that equalled or exceeded the mortgage debt. In some cases, this took more than a decade after purchase.

Capital-based, property-based strategies are especially exposed when the tide goes out. Similar to the ills that the average property developer faces when transactions slow as the market gums up, those who don't have an income-based strategy will feel the heat most when the market turns. These types of strategies, such as owning holiday homes in the sun that don't rent out or high-end swanky apartments in city centres that have low yields, can be a favourite to sell to inexperienced investors. One-off capital gains can look much more appealing than income from property because of the much bigger numbers involved. Some may believe it's better to make £100,000 from capital gains from owning a flat over five years, rather than taking 'just' £10,000 a year in net income. I would take the income any day as it will probably drop into the account automatically without the need to swap time for money, and will probably keep arriving for the rest of my life.

I regularly see people enter into property development projects without doing their sums correctly. Usually excited by potential profits, they regularly include all the costs of the development project and miss items like finance interest, professional fees, groundworks/ conditions, cost of roofs, windows, insulation and planning issues that need to be factored in.

15

What really works in business, finance and investing

Most of what I believe works in business, finance and investing goes against the tide, and is uncommon sense. While some of these points may have been touched upon, here are some specific areas in business, finance and investing that have rewarded me with success and profit.

Short-term challenges

I love investing in companies that the media has had a good go at. When the media starts an onslaught of criticism of a company on a near daily basis, this is the time to start tracking it. It's perhaps not the best idea to start investing too early before the venom has really started to flow: the skill is working out when interest in denigrating the said company has reached its hiatus. Clearly, you would only focus on companies you believe are solid long-term performers able to weather the storm, and which have good products you understand, with balance sheets and profitability to match. Once they are trading off what looks to be a reasonable profit-to-earnings ratio relative to others in their sector, it might be time to pounce.

British Petroleum, Tesco and Volkswagen have all been victims of consistent media attacks, largely because of a specific event that harmed their profitability or reputation. Once this kind of thing happens, many investors will press the sell button and ask questions later, not wanting to be invested at times of volatility. A second tier of investors will be further influenced by the daily negative press, and their emotions will likely push them to sell without conducting further research. As long as you believe in the long-term fundamentals of businesses such as these, the share price will often outperform the market once the issue and subsequently media interest passes or turns more positive.

Understandable

When choosing which assets, classes and businesses to invest in, it is a good idea to pick ones that banks understand, like and can secure their money against. Most income-producing property meets this criterion, but as soon as it becomes non-mainstream such as a lease-hold house or equities based on a lesser-known exchange like AIM, there will be much less interest from banks wanting to lend. Careful leverage can also be applied to funds that hold equity and bond-based investments. Barclays Wealth offers such a facility, lending around 60 per cent against a portfolio they manage. This leverage can provide more interesting returns, especially coupled with low-interest rates. As your relationship improves and the funds you put with these banks increase, you will end up with lower rates, too. The more off the beaten track your model or class is, the less the banks like it and therefore the less you are able to leverage and grow.

Balanced

With any portfolio, it is important to have a spread of different asset types and classes to protect and diversify your income streams. When further into the macroeconomic cycle, it is usually a good idea to protect this downside by investing in less cyclically affected businesses like house-building companies and banks (unless you think they are particularly cheap or mispriced). Your attitude to risk, age, net worth, disposable income and perhaps knowledge will determine your spread of these assets.

Someone like me will be overweight compared to most on property, because this is the asset class I focus on and understand best. I like to have a portion of my investments in higher-risk individual equities (usually up to 5 per cent of net worth), which I believe have a short-term issue or are cheap for some reason. The rest of my ISA funds almost all go into long-term funds managed by quality managers who have outperformed over the long term. The rest is spread between trading businesses, property, cash and physical assets. Clearly, if you see a crash coming it would be a good idea to be heavier on cash and physical assets and perhaps equities in counter-cyclical businesses such as utilities, discount retailers and letting agencies.

Clean credit

Keeping a clean credit history with which the banks judge you is a critical part of being able to raise funds for investment. This applies personally and in your businesses. While many will want to raise funds for business or other investments, as my focus is property, convincing banks to lend money to me is key to being able to invest and obtain leverage on the projects that will create further growth. As you can borrow on buildings at 2–4 per cent (2016), which might produce a net yield/income of 8 per cent, your margin is 4–6 per cent on the income. If most of this money is borrowed, you have just created an income stream with around 30 per cent of your own money left in the investment. I can't overstate the power of this.

As your credit history is like a CV to the bank, any blemishes may increase the rate or harm the terms you get from them, or at worst lead to a refusal for a loan. And as leverage is one of the keys to making market-outperforming money in property, the long-term effects of having a poor credit history can be huge, due to the effect of compounding.

- Make sure you repay in full all your bills and credit cards each month via direct debit so you don't miss them.
- Register with the council to get you on the electoral roll and make sure you log into Experian credit expert regularly to ensure that nothing is happening that you don't know about.

- Monitor, or have your financial director monitor, all issues or threats to the creditworthiness of your companies. Commercial lenders and venture capitalists are especially interested in the company rather than your personal score, but the principle remains the same: guard your score with your life as the long-term costs of having a low score can be very high.

New(ish) innovations

It seems that many futurists are predicting that VR (virtual reality) and AI (artificial intelligence) are models for the future. All this is still a little speculative and unproven for me, so I will watch with interest to see how these disruptive technologies and models fare. I can see the vast scale and mass appeal of VR, as it can be used across existing web, net and social platforms almost instantaneously. IOT (the Internet of Things) seems to be gaining momentum, and it is not so Orwellian to think that most products will have chips or net access for data accrual and speed/ease of use. While today it may seem gimmicky to access the Internet from your fridge, the benefits of automation, updates and real-time data exchange are potentially massive. IOT, VR and AI all seem to dovetail and so these could be the future of business and innovation. I am sure some speculators will make big gains, but I like to see a little more track record.

16

Challenges we all face in business, finance and investing

Many business, finance and investing mistakes are driven by emotion, perhaps nearly all of them. We react to our emotions instead of being in control of them, and while they serve a purpose for survival, they can make investors and business owners seem like hormonal teenagers. The first stage is simply to be aware of your emotions, looking at your reactions as if you are a different person giving yourself feedback: 'Oh, Mark, that's an interesting reaction to that occurrence.' The second and third stages of controlling these emotions are discussed in the last section of this book.

Going in too deep or too fast

Some people have the habit of making financial decisions that don't serve them and that can harm their long-term financial wellbeing. Many of these poor decisions become noteworthy because significant investments are made before a period of testing is concluded. With property, especially when developing new strategies, it is important to make the first investments and wait for the results. Property investments, specifically, take six to 12 months to properly show their face and provide accurate data. Only then can they be relied upon for making future investment decisions. Most of the refinement and improvement of the process, which reduces the number of mistakes next time around, come from this period of enlightenment. And this is where most of my mistakes, and other people's I have observed, have come from: going in too fast without a testing period or too deep so that the mistakes cost too much money.

Over-excitement and fear

Over-exuberance or excitement can also lead to poor financial and commercial decisions. As discussed in the early chapters of this book, the herd mentality can encourage less experienced investors to jump in and make decisions based on what others collectively think is the right thing to do. They follow the herd rather than making decisions for themselves based on research, testing and measuring. We all want to feel good and to be seen in a good light, so we appease these feel-good emotions rather than the colder reality.

Fear investing and decision-making can also be damaging. I frequently read articles from certain publications or individuals on social media about how the property market (or some other market) is about to implode. At the bottom of their article, they promote the solution to the fear that they have just spread. Clearly, they have an ulterior motive and their comments should be taken with a large dose of salt. Others follow the same process, with threats of legal consequences should a particular strategy be followed. They then try to sell their solution, which they claim to be more legally valid or lower risk than the process they castigated. The reality is that the original strategy didn't carry the purported risk, but the reader bought into it and was persuaded to buy a different financial product, mortgage or the like.

Letting it all out

The temptation in business (and life in general) is often to let your feelings be known, especially when you feel that someone has been unfair, caused you a big issue, lied to you or perhaps that a member of staff ignored your instructions. You want them to 'have it'. Nothing is achieved by becoming emotional or by letting these raw feelings blurt out all over the place without due care and thought. It will usually put in you a worse position with the other person, and trigger negative emotional responses from them. This will only make your interactions and negotiations more difficult and probably less fruitful. Getting angry can often satisfy an emotional need and be cathartic, but it is best saved until later, when you are somewhere else. Sitting on it, thinking about it, isolating yourself away from other people, talking to someone you trust and respect about it are all strategies that can help. Exercise is a great way to relieve pent-up emotions, too.

A specific example of what not to do when things go wrong is the time we bought an management system to check in and manage delegates at an event. Each delegate would be given a lanyard upon arrival with a bar code with which they would be scanned into the building. Each time they wanted to buy a product, their lanyard would be scanned and their credit card details used to pay for the course or an item. Promised that the system would work seamlessly, we decided to install and implement it at our property super-conference at Wembley Stadium. With around 1,000 people attending, it seemed a good way to keep the delegates organized and reduce queuing times. Little did we know …

As soon as we opened the doors, the system started to go wrong. The label printers malfunctioned and a queue of 600 people formed outside the front door in the cold weather. They were not happy and understandably getting upset. As the architect of the system had conveniently disappeared for the afternoon, it caused a fiasco, with customers becoming fed up before the event had even started.

Eventually, we started to sign people in manually, as we had done previously, and the queue reduced. As people came in, the event started and they calmed down. Most forgot about the issue, except for me. I was livid. After repeated specific assurances from the developer of the system about it being reliable and him being on hand to deal with any issues, he wasn't present and it had cost us dearly in customer experience, goodwill and ultimately sales.

When the owner of the business arrived, I confronted him about his deficient system. He protested that most of it was our fault. I was so angry with him that I couldn't hold it in and let rip, going berserk at him in one of the side alleys around the stadium. This made him even more defensive and achieved very little. We ended up in protracted legal negotiations, stuck with a system that didn't work and out of pocket. What I should have done was dealt with him firmly but calmly, negotiating in a way that allowed him to save face. This would probably have resulted in a better outcome for both of us.

Chopping and changing

So many people I meet have a need always to be trying something new. They have some emotional need that is satisfied by trying new things. Perhaps the excitement of the dream is more pleasing than the reality of the money. Sure, this need for variety exists in most of us, but too much variety leads to a lot of nothing. When you start a new business in an area that is unrelated to that of the one you have exited early, everything gets reset to zero, including all your knowledge, customers, goodwill, brand, mind space, referrals, marketing, web assets and all the other intangible but valuable things that took time to build. These are the things that the average person doesn't see when blinded by the excitement of possibility over reality. All the mistakes you made and learned from, the costs incurred from making them and solving them, and the entire investment of time, money and energy in the iterative process of becoming successful and profitable, all reset to zero.

As much as some believe otherwise, the grass is rarely greener in another business that you don't understand. Virtually all models and classes have similar or the very same challenges and entrance fees. To think it will somehow be easier, quicker and better and that all your current problems will go away with this one change is delusional.

Obviously, if you have been in employment and not had a business before, you will need to make a change decision. Just don't make it a habit you repeat every six months, or when the first business seems too much like hard work. All businesses take hard work. Make these big life-changing decisions infrequently and with the care and attention they deserve. In business and investing, once you are up and running, in nearly all cases, the best decision is to carry on with what you are doing, and just get better at it. Also, remember that others are experiencing exactly the same thoughts and feelings as you about their businesses. You are not alone, it is normal, and most other people are likely to give up the longer you are in your business or asset.

> It is far better to go slow for the full distance than to go fast and hard but burn out.

17
Time saving versus time investing

I love saving time and carrying out tasks more efficiently. I welcome any task I can perform that can be leveraged for a longer period of time or over a larger amount of purchases or sales. For example, when I lived alone, I would buy a two-year supply of all non-perishable items in the house. By compiling a spreadsheet covering toothpaste, shampoo, shaving foam, razors, bin liners, dishwasher tablets, batteries, washing powder and so on, I could calculate my usage of all these items over a two-year period. Then, I would save time and money by buying a two-year supply of everything in the house in January when they were cheap.

I bought 60 shirts and 12 suits so that I could make a bi-monthly trip to the dry cleaners, again saving significant time and money. I have transplanted this thinking to many of the tasks that I perform in business, finance and investing. Systemizing tasks is key to making progress – distilling them on to a spreadsheet or checklist to reduce the amount of time they take.

I like to outsource most business and personal tasks that I'm not good at or interested in. Another example would be clothes shopping, which I absolutely hate. I have leveraged such tasks out to my fiancée, Gemma, who will pick items for me to wear when we are out shopping. I try them on and then make a quick purchase decision. Choosing clothes to wear each morning is something that gives me decision fatigue, so Gemma will pick my clothes out on non-work days, saving us both time. It also means that I look respectable to her and vaguely presentable in public, rather than the mess I would make as a left-brain thinker.

My mind operates better when dealing with logic or mathematical subject matter. Because of this, I seem to have naturally surrounded myself with more right-brain, creative thinkers. Gemma is certainly one of these and finds interior design, fashion and most aspects of creative thinking much easier than I do. This is one of the reasons I outsource most of the interior design of our projects to her, as this is what she excels in. I realize that some may find me somewhat strange, but you can model the principle of outsourcing the things you don't enjoy to other people. Save that time and reinvest it into income-generating tasks or simply to save and free your time. My saving grace is knowing that Steve Jobs wore his infamous jeans, trainers and black turtleneck not to build a recognizable brand, as most people think, but so that he didn't have to waste his time choosing clothes to buy and to wear.

Another area of my life that I like to save time on is IT. We have various systems in our business that collate and manage data, which significantly reduce paper-based operations and ensure that items are easily collatable. We use Infusionsoft as a contact manager, which collates and sends emails, takes payments and stores notes on customers. We use the CFPwinMan property management system to manage the rental properties handled by our letting agency. Sage is a good tool for managing the finance side of our business, and is well understood by finance staff and external tax accountants. It provides detailed understandable accounts to the management team, which enables us to make quick decisions to enhance the business.

The switch from physical paper-based books to audiobooks has been profound. I regularly drive to work listening to an audio-book on a topic relating to business or improving my life through higher-quality relationships or food and exercise. This 'no extra time' (NeTime) time-saving mechanism makes journeys more interesting and allows me to feel I'm not wasting my time when driving. It's amazing how many of these books you can get through on journeys. Clearly, taking action and implementing the concepts raised in the books afterward is crucial.

I used to believe that saving money was paramount over all else, but I'm now cognisant of the need to value my time. I often do a calculation where I take my yearly income and divide it by the num-ber of working hours in that year based on a nine-hour day. I will then arrive at an hourly figure. I use this figure to work out whether the task I'm doing is a good use of my time or best leveraged to somebody else. Since really living this concept, I now have a cleaner, a personal PA and a full-time researcher. In addition, all properties are managed by a business in which I have a shareholding but which is run by my business partner. Most development projects are now outsourced to a main contractor, and many properties are purchased through an in-house buyer who finds them. I'm very much of the belief that even small products that reduce my time wastage, such as my high-street bank all-in-one account that provides travel insurance, mobile phone cover, RAC cover and so on, are great as I don't need to search around for the best deal each year.

I reinvest the time saved in these areas into others areas that are more compatible with left-brain thought. This, in turn, allows me to reap bigger rewards for our business. I'm naturally better at these more analytical tasks. Much property investment utilizes left-brain thought (analysis, research, details), which is one of the reasons I think it became my calling. Having another 30 minutes in the morning will mean that I can read another contract, look at another property investment deal or make another contact at a bank that will provide returns multiple times over. These compounded time savings make a significant difference when leveraged over many years. I just have to sanity-check every now and again that I am not getting too sucked into time saving, whereas right-brain thinkers may have to do the opposite.

Part 3: Strategies and tactics

In this section, we will discuss specific strategies that I know from experience work well and generate sustained profit in business, finance and investing, with a leaning towards profiting by going against the tide. I'll start with overriding strategies and then drill down into some very specific tactics so that you have applicable techniques that you can implement in your business and investments.

You might find me moving, apparently randomly, between a higher-level concept and an analytical detail in finance. I will also reference mentors and investors for whom I have great admiration, mainly for their enduring success.

18

Four overriding strategies for investment

Every investment goes through its own cycles and counter-cycles, and so offers value or is overpriced at different stages within its own cycle. This is independent of other classes. These cycles are just like plates spinning at different speeds, some slowing down, some just starting to spin and speed up, and you balancing them all. For some classes, the asset is fundamentally solid but the timing is wrong. For others, the time is now but will not last so you need to jump in. You may need deep, competition-beating knowledge in three to five classes to be able to rotate your investments, diversify enough but go deep at the right time in a single class, and there's a limit to what you can know, do and invest personally.

To balance this, there are four overriding strategies for investment (time, money, business model):

1 Invest yourself.
2 Be a partner in a joint venture (JV).
3 Outsource.
4 Do nothing.

1 Invest yourself

You will gain the deepest knowledge, experience and competition-outsmarting results if you focus your time and energy in a specific business model or class, making it your passion-profession. This is, of course, obvious, but you are less able to do this if you spread yourself too thinly or if you are unsure of your vision for your business and your life. Pick a class or model that you enjoy doing: if it seems like less like work, you will not need power-motivation to do it. It doesn't matter too much which class or model this is as long as it has proven commercial and historical residuals. The closer to the best you become, the more you can monetize it compared to a seemingly better class with limited knowledge. You should focus 50–70 per cent of your time on this single class or model. Of course, you can't do this for three to five classes, which is where the next three overriding strategies come in.

2 Be a partner in a joint venture (JV)

For another class or model, you can partner with someone who operates the first strategy. I learned all about watches from my business partner, Rob Moore, and while I have some enjoyment, I much prefer to leverage his knowledge, experience, research and passion, and either invest with him or take his recommendations. And he does the reverse with me in property. There are upsides and downsides of this strategy versus No. 1, and it is not a case of one being better than the other. It is more a case of deciding which strategy you will use for which class and model.

You are smart to JV with people who have different interests and focus on different niches from you, but who have a similar, long-term vision so you are not (re)starting with new partners every year. You can leverage each other and the trust you create over time. The upside is time and financial leverage; the downsides can be letting go of control and decision-making, and vulnerability or exposure to more risk.

3 Outsource

This is where you use a passive investment such as a fund, a loan (secured) or individual stock. These are lower-risk, lower-return investments and, as such, usually create a more passive return. If you invest in regulated investments and/or use fund managers, time is taken up front with your research and due diligence, but after that you do very little to sustain the return, other than checks and maintenance. Other areas where you can outsource your investing at a higher risk and return are growing your business and hiring more staff, using your capital for buying businesses, lending money and crowdfunding.

4 Do nothing

Strangely, for many people this seems to be the hardest one to master. They either do nothing at all, which gets them nowhere, or they don't know when it is the right time to do nothing and their activity and impatience cost them time and money. You need to know and balance when to do nothing because the time is wrong to do something, and when to do something because you are doing nothing. If you are to agree that three to five classes or models is about the right level, and you are balancing Nos. 1–3 above (invest yourself, JV, outsource), then there will be models you have to say no to, despite being tempted by the masses or something that comes at the right time but is the wrong thing.

I find it quite easy to assume that new things need to be handled with caution until proven otherwise, and I like to see sustained proof before taking on risk. However, I observe that many people just can't help themselves, can't sit on their hands, are impatient or get sucked in by media hype, over-excitement or impatience. A way to control this is to say 'Yes, but not now.' Put the decision on ice and revisit it later, so that you never actually have to say a definite 'No', if that is something you find hard to do.

In order to preserve and maximize your time, take the time to get good enough yourself in some areas, but remain open to gaining benefit from the skills and experience of others. You need to balance all four of these overriding strategies of how and where you invest your time and funds. One area is possibly too risky, five may be too thinly diversified. But you are also dependent on what is working at a particular time, what you have an interest in yourself, and the partners and network you have access to, and so this is a constantly changing equation.

19

Regulated versus unregulated investing

Regulated investments are approved and controlled by the regulatory authorities of the respective countries. Many aspects of the investment are controlled in the way they are run, valued, promoted and marketed, sold and externally audited. In order to sell a regulated investment, you would need to be a regulated adviser or company and compliant with many rules and processes.

The major upside of regulated investments or companies regulated for investment is the protection it gives you from poorly run schemes or scams. With regulated investments, an investment needs to be proven and sustainable to meet the strict regulations required. The vehicles are almost always financially solvent and therefore the risk is reduced.

The major drawback of regulated investments is the very low returns. Even with the most impressive regulated investments, medium single-digit returns are the best-case scenario, and returns are often even lower. It is clear to me that many such investments continue to offer low returns partly because they are regulated. After having gained this badge, they attract the interest of many more consumers and so competition is reduced. As an entrepreneur or business owner, if you made these percentage returns you'd feel it was hardly worth the time, effort and risk to set up in the first place.

Now, it is important to note that one investment type is not actually better than another. When you are less experienced, regulated investments keep you safer and provide more predictable, likely returns than unregulated ones. The irony of this is that you have less capital and you want/need higher returns. As you become more experienced, your ability to get higher returns and mitigate the risk increases, and the attraction of downside protection as a trade-off for low relative returns diminishes.

While it is not my desire to define a stereotyped strategy, I like to have assets, capital and businesses in both regulated and unregulated vehicles. This enables a spread of assets and income streams across different vehicles, classes and styles at different levels of risk.

Here are some of the reasons I hold regulated investments:

1 To de-risk overexposure in a single asset class
2 To mitigate the damage of a single one going wrong
3 As a way to hold cash and wait for a higher-return, unregulated investment
4 For liquidity
5 For more passive investments or to build passive income streams.

Here are some reasons I hold unregulated investments:

1 To seek (vastly) higher returns
2 For control*
3 To save fees
4 Because no one will manage your investment better than you
5 To become educated and experienced in a class or business model.

In addition, I like to have a balance of the two areas to negate or reduce the downsides and get the benefit of as many of the upsides as I can.

*Important note: In the main, I do not invest in unregulated investments that I don't directly control. In my experience, investing in schemes that others control and that are not regulated is a recipe for losses. This is because it is much harder to protect an asset or investment that is unregulated if it is under the control of someone else.

If you are new to investing or have little capital, it is wise to start investing safely at first in regulated investments such as investment funds, bonds and equities if the bank rates are good. Once you have some disposable capital, you can make higher-risk and potentially higher-return investments yourself that are unregulated. You will win some and lose some. As you make money in the some that win, you should reinvest part of the profit into regulated investments to build a protective war chest that can serve as a pension or to future-proof your position. As you build that capital base, it can produce income that has a very low risk of drying up because the capital is ring-fenced. Simultaneously, you educate yourself on unregulated investments and businesses that have higher risk return for the bigger, more speculative and 'lumpy' profits (and sometimes losses).

Then, as your capital and income come in multiple streams and become big enough, you can play around with your ratios between the two. If rates are very low, you may want less capital in regulated investments, for example, and vice versa if rates are high. If you have capital waiting while you are looking for other assets that have a long sourcing time frame (such as buying commercial property or businesses), this would likely sit in a liquid, low-return regulated investment. If it is a buyer's market in a particular class, you might want a larger percentage of your capital in unregulated classes.

20

My investing strategies

My ideal holding period is for ever. I like the concept of putting the work in once, even if it takes a little longer than desired, expected or compared to others, and the asset paying you for the rest of your life with a small amount of maintenance and spot-checking. This probably fits with my accumulator personality type. Constantly selling assets to buy more has transactional costs and time costs. When money can be borrowed cheaply against a percentage of the assets you already hold, I'm not sure why you would be in the selling mindset. Warren Buffet has a similar philosophy with shares: as long as the asset has not materially changed or there's a good reason for selling (and there can be from time to time), he won't sell.

I like to stay within my sphere of understanding, business model or asset class. When going into a new investing or business area, I like to know that it is related or not too far away from what I already know or do. This saves time, reduces the risk of making assumptions that turn out to be untrue, and usually allows you to plug the operation into your existing architecture. You get dove-tailed, crossover benefit, like having hundreds of properties and then starting up a letting agency. Using your existing infrastructure or customer base to launch into something will usually create much better results and leverage time already invested rather than setting the clock back to zero. Much of the testing and measuring have been done on the core part of the idea and you only need to learn, test and measure the last 20 per cent or so. Other examples might be going into hotels when you are already into houses in multiple occupation (HMOs), starting a personal training business when you are already a personal trainer, or setting up a franchise around your existing business model.

My criteria for investing

When investing in stocks, property and other asset classes, I like to buy under the following criteria:

1 An asset with an issue that others can't solve but I can
2 A strong asset or stock that is enduring short-term challenges (but with proven history and very low chances of going under)
3 A seller with cash flow or other issues and motivated to sell
4 Post-recession, bust or undervalued part of the cycle (not always clear)
5 Changing the use/function of an asset/investment.

1 An asset with an issue that others can't solve but I can

If there is a leasehold issue that my solicitor can solve, an absentee freeholder or title issue that I have previous experience of solving, or a planning challenge I can work around, these are examples of issues that may be problematic to vendors but not to me. I am able to extract value and then increase the value once the problem is solved. This is much like a watchmaker who can repair a defective watch at a wholesale price and then sell it to the retail market. The more I know about an asset class, the more these opportunities arise. I am careful not to go into investments with issues in asset classes I don't fully understand. In these cases, the existing problem can become my problem and I've essentially bought a liability. Ugly houses, non-sexy stocks, and old, nondescript watches are examples of assets that most people miss because they don't glisten; I quite like them.

2 A strong asset or stock that is enduring short-term challenges

This is my main investing strategy when picking stocks of individual companies. I am not a trader, although I am often tempted to fiddle around with my portfolio. I do like to buy into a fundamentally good company with short-term issues that have reduced its value for the short term. While I am not recommending these, previous examples have included Coca-Cola when health warnings come out, Volkswagen and other car manufacturers when emissions scandals broke out, developers and banks in post-recession periods (as long as they are big proven ones and not challenger or boutique banks with a shorter history) or shorting the dollar with news of Brexit. The bad news reduces their stock price but, fundamentally, I feel that they will recover and the likelihood of them going bust is very, very low. When I buy in, I will pound-cost-average, which is buying in stages at different times and prices in order to reduce risk.

3 A seller with cash flow or other issues and motivated to sell

If the seller has motivations or challenges, they will accept a reduced price for liquidity (fast purchase, helping clear debt). These motivated sellers are more common in times of recession, but people experience challenges through all parts of the cycle. You can help people out of sticky situations and get assets at reduced market prices.

4 Post-recession, during the undervalued part of the cycle

The best time to buy is when a market is at its most bare. You can't predict with accuracy when this will happen, or time the bottom of the market, but you can stockpile cash while the going is good and be ready to invest heavily when you are confident that prices and confidence are about as low as they will go. One of those periods of time in the property market was 2009/10. I am glad to say we were relatively well capitalized when this hit. I often yearn for those times with nostalgia and wish I had bought up my entire city, including the cathedral; it would have been perfect for a flatted development!

5 Changing the use/function of an asset/investment

If you can buy an asset that the market and the competition see only in its existing use, and you can add value to the asset by changing the use, then you can create value. An example may be to take a disused building and turn it into apartments or rooms, or to take a company that isn't making much profit and change the market or product. Some people with enterprise are even taking high-end watches and adding gemstones to them, or taking phones and coating them with high-end materials and selling them at a profit. As with any investment, you should do this only if you have knowledge and experience.

Traps to avoid

I do not like to invest under the following criteria (that the masses do):

1 There are inherent issues that cannot be fixed.
2 Everyone is talking up the stock or asset (such as a hotspot or popular tech company).

These need no explanation at all; you know by now that the uncommon sense philosophy is to mostly ignore the masses.

I would like to point out some uncommon sense views to some commonly held beliefs and strategies around business, investing and finance:

The sunk cost trap

This is a common mistake that investors make, where they have invested significant funds (and time and energy) into something and become welded to it. If, over a period of time, it becomes clear that the investment won't be profitable or meet your investment objectives, it is time to eat humble pie and dump it. Many investors will stick with the investment, as it is emotionally less painful to do so, even though if they were really honest they know that the investment isn't good. Not only do these investors suffer bad returns, but they also lose out in the opportunity cost of the money. The opportunity cost would be the higher returns that they would have experienced elsewhere with a well-performing investment. In addition, the mental and emotional benefit of cutting your ties with a negative investment that affects your head space and prevents other opportunities from receiving the consideration they deserve, is significant. Cut them loose and experience the freedom this creates.

Only judge an investment on its merits and not on the financial, time or energy investment. The opposite can sometimes be true if an investment has done well with little time or energy. In these instances, don't sell it just because you didn't think the returns earned were deserved. Time and energy already spent have no bearing on the future outcome, so leave them behind.

When to change – and when to keep going

Even though it's important to invest for the long term, remain steadfast to your beliefs and strategies and to not chop and change every five minutes, it is also important to reflect and pivot when absolutely necessary. Many investors become anchored to certain beliefs about certain companies that were good performers but, due to a structural or market change, are no longer so. It is OK to change your mind about a business model or investment, or product choice, partner or marketing strategy, if it is the right thing to do. Once you are sure and it has been given due consideration consistently over a period of time, commit to changing your actions. Know when to keep going (most of the time) and when to pivot (when the market or circumstances dictate it).

Avoiding pain

The emotional negativity that bad investments create can cause investors and business owners to avoid dealing with them. They bury their head in the sand because it is easier to remove the pain by ignoring it, pretending that it isn't there or that isn't that big a deal. While this strategy makes people feel better in the short term, it doesn't help them understand what has gone wrong and/or learn from it. 'No pain, no gain' may be a platitude but is true for all that. Hold your breath, take some initially painful steps that will arrest the harm that an investment or decision is doing to your business or portfolio, and you will more quickly solve the problem. And, just as valuably, you will harvest great lessons that you can 'reinvest' into future decisions.

If you leave something that stinks in the corner of your bedroom, the smell is likely to get worse and worse until you have a real problem getting rid of it. Honesty about your investments is very liberating, and will often mean that the more experienced people around you will believe and respect you more. You become a powerful force to yourself and others, an indispensable asset, when you are known for getting stuck in and solving problems fast.

Superiority complex

Many investors can fall into a trap where they believe that they are superior or more intelligent than the rest of the market. Being well educated or experienced in a market may help, but a healthy awareness of your fallibility and some humility will keep you sustainable and open to lessons and new experiences.

Extremes

Humans are imperfect creatures that succumb to psychological stress and heightened emotions when things are going really well, or very badly. We tend to see things only in extreme polar opposites, rather than the constant balance of both extremes in any situation. Things are never as bad as they seem, or as good as they seem. If you are focused on one part of the balance emotional equation, you will not see the reality that is there. Everything has an upside and a downside. So stay calm when it seems that things are not going well. Do not make rash decisions and look for the upside to balance your emotions. Often, in times of hardship, you will find valuable lessons, resilience, new opportunities and experience. It can be good to sleep on a decision and, after giving yourself time to consider it, ensure that you are feeling good or more balanced when making the decision.

Decisions made in haste or in the wrong emotional state (too low and too high) can be costly and are often regretted later.

21

Profiting by going against the tide

Big money can be made in times of change in the economy by going against big swings in the value of assets. Many people fear change, but the biggest changes or corrections produce the greatest opportunities. At times like this, when the economy goes into reverse, people become fearful and the value of gold generally rises. The general public usually then starts to hear about the merits of investing in something a few years after it has had a very good run. As gold hadn't been talked about much before the 2007 financial crisis, it didn't appear in the forefront of public consciousness for a few years afterwards. Gold shops then appeared on most high streets, advertisements to sell gold seemed to appear everywhere, and people started to search their loft spaces for gold that was lying around to cash it in, often at poor rates.

The reality was that many of the investors who bought gold (largely on the exchanges) bought when the price had been elevated due to market uncertainty and investors' need for a safe haven. By the time 2015 came around, gold had dropped again, and the weight of money that had originally come into the asset (from largely novice investors who bought in a couple of years after gold rose, after the credit crunch of 2010) was largely gone. Spotting an opportunity in late 2015, and with the UK's referendum looming on whether to stay in the European Union, it became clear to George Soros that uncertainty pre-vote (and perhaps post-vote, as actually happened) would return and gold would rise again. News of his big bet didn't come out until later, but his 20-per-cent-plus return became clear.

Soros had done again what he did in the 1992 exchange rate mechanism debacle, a European system that effectively pegged sterling to the much-admired Deutschmark managed by the Bundesbank. With inflation and growth rates out of kilter between the two countries, and a mismatched initial entry exchange rate, Black Wednesday came about when the UK government attempted to beat traders who were selling the pound. The Conservatives (who at that time set interest rates rather than the Bank of England) bought sterling aggressively, and interest rates rose to 12 per cent and for a short period reached 15 per cent. In the end, Soros and many other traders who were selling the pound won when the UK government decided they couldn't commit more funds. These investors profited by going against the tide and made hundreds of millions by playing the contrarians.

Lessons from mentors and investors

The investors I mention below aren't necessarily contrarian for the sake of being contrarian, but are so by nature of having succeeded in the long term when most others have not.

Andreas Panayiotou

The residential property market has gone up in value multiple times more than its commercial counterpart over the past 50 years. In some areas, such as London, you can add a zero on to the percentage growth rate for residential property capital values versus commercial as a result of the huge demand-side pressure which has come from a ballooning population and lack of supply. Andreas Panayiotou made the right call here by choosing to house people rather than businesses. He eventually sold his portfolio in 2006 to a City fund, after he had become the largest private-sector residential landlord in the country, with 8,000 flats. His timing was impeccable as the market crash started at the end of 2007. He then went into hotels, performing a series of deals with the likes of the Hilton and Radisson groups, buying the freehold and having them run the hotels under a management contract.

Panayiotou started out in the East End of London in his parents' dry cleaning shop. He noticed that old commercial buildings were either empty or under-utilized as mansion houses containing flats. In time, he bought up commercial buildings and converted them into blocks of flats and then, unlike most other developers who were mainly selling their developments, he profited by going against the tide and renting them out. Holding these investments for a long period, then leveraging bank debt at low rates, has meant that he has effectively gained from the capital growth when he initially converted the flats. But he has also gained year on year as the market has gone up in value.

Some of the lessons I have learned from him have been invaluable. He is a great proponent of adding value and entering into property investments only where a buffer can be created. He would then always leverage (but to a sensible 60–70-per-cent level) from one of the big commercial lenders. He would usually only invest where gross yields are in the 6 to 8-per-cent-plus range.

Warren Buffett

Another investor I respect a great deal, who has also profited by going against the tide, is Warren Buffett. His story is well known as to become slightly clichéd and he seems largely uninterested in the trappings of wealth. He does, however, spend huge amounts of time reading company financial reports and getting to know company operations, management and prospects. I respect the way he ignores much of what the herd is investing in and sticks to businesses that he understands deeply.

This became very obvious around the tech boom of 1997–2000. Buffett consistently refused to jump in and invest, unlike most other market participants (including myself). He said that he didn't understand technology companies; they were outside his circle of competence, so he sat on his hands. This was probably not easy to do when everyone was jumping in and when, from the outside, it looked like a licence to print money, but is a perfect example of the uncommon sense philosophy. The fact that most of these companies had little historical data on which to base investment decisions was also a problem. When a company doesn't have a proven concept or profit, stock market valuations can be crazy and share prices can go up 20 times in one day (yes, this has occurred – I invested in some of them in my late teens). Of course, that is only obvious now with hindsight.

Buffett's attention to detail from an early age has served him well; he began reading business and investment books in his early teens. This archetypal 'geek' drives a £40,000 Cadillac XTS and lives in a house he purchased for about £20,000 in 1958, all of which would not be out of the reach of many normal American families. To me, there is something endearing about how he knows himself enough to know that material items don't do it for him, and his contrarian fabric allows him to ignore the yachts and Bugattis that society says he should have. That is not to say that someone shouldn't have these items if they genuinely enjoy them, but I admire people a little more if they pick and choose things in life because they love them rather than because they believe society expects them to.

Anthony Bolton

Another seasoned investor who has profited by going against the tide and who got my attention in the mid-2000s was Anthony Bolton, the famous stock picker who ran the Fidelity Special Situations fund. He followed some rather simple but clearly effective principles:

1 Know why you own a stock.
2 Know what's discounted in the price.
3 Know yourself.

Bolton is another example of an investor who, having largely ignored the dotcom stocks of the early 2000s, is very much one for standing apart from the crowd. His assertion is that it is important to invest in companies that you know something about. A doctor investing in a medical company is much better than one investing in a tin-mining operation. In addition to this, it is important to understand if and to what extent you believe the market has mispriced a company's stock.

Since the market is a representation of what people *believe* the future holds rather than the reality of what the future holds, it is often wrong. If you want to profit from stocks, it is your job to spot this mispricing in areas and with companies you understand. Should market participants be generally negative about the market's prospects after a crash, with bearish sentiment being popular, many companies will offer attractive valuations. A critical lesson is that Bolton believes that when there are still plenty of cautious investors around, the market probably still has further to go.

Neil Woodford

Neil Woodford is another well-publicized investor who has a long track record of success in the stock market, and is someone I believe has profited by going against the tide. Again, focusing his attention on areas he thoroughly understands, he often homes in on companies with higher than average dividend or income yields. Making sure these are sustainable and not here today and gone tomorrow, he has built his funds to provide some of the most consistently good returns for many decades.

A consistent theme in his investment pattern is investing in tobacco companies. Citing that his job is to make his investors good returns rather than make ethical judgements, he has focused part of his funds on cigarette manufacturers, as he noticed their unusually high dividend income yields. As many investors won't buy tobacco companies because of the damage these products can inflict, the capital value or share price of many of these companies has become abnormally depressed. For Woodford, herein lies an opportunity for a classical contrarian to profit by going against the tide.

Applying the lessons

We have had some good results by going against the tide too, in our own humble way. Between 2009 and 2011, we went on a shopping spree, buying up UK commercial properties with the intention of converting them into residential properties. Calling on our years of expertise and gut feeling, we assessed the state of the market. Many commercial buildings had dropped in value in excess of 80 per cent of their 2007 value, so we went in aggressively because we thought prices couldn't get much lower.

With the media constantly reminding people of how wounded property had become, the mood became very negative. As we had invested heavily pre-recession, we would get many people offering sympathy and condolences and we would be questioned on how bad things were for our business, with many assuming that things were tough for everyone in the property market. In fact, the rental market strengthened during this period as fewer people were able or wanted to purchase homes. As rents rose, so did profits. Clearly, capital values suffered, but this only really affected those who had to sell, such as developers. As is usually the case, this negativity was at it highest in most people's minds in 2009 and 2010, when it was ironically the best time to be buying. As our mindset was perfectly aligned to the uncommon sense philosophy, we were in a perfect position to profit against the tide.

By 2013, the media and the wider public had turned much more positive on property, after the biggest recovery had already taken place. Most of the assets we bought during the bear period quickly increased in value by over 30 per cent, producing multiple millions in capital growth. Prices rise in a recovery just as quickly as they drop in a recession. The negativity in the media really helped our investing as it eroded confidence, so we are grateful to them for that, and as usual listening to the masses could have been very damaging to our wealth.

There will be many people telling you what you should and shouldn't do in your business and investments. We were told that live events would be dead as soon as online streaming gained momentum. We were told our training business would be disrupted by free social media. We got 'advice' from all over the place, mostly from people motivated to hold us back. We rarely sought this advice but had it imposed upon us by those with no experience in making sustained profits. Remember that free advice is worth every penny – as long as it comes from the right source. Ensure that you are only taking advice from people who have been there and done it for a sustained period of time. There is no need to get into heavy debates and waste your time. Simply smile, thank them for their advice, and carry on doing exactly what you were doing. On the other hand, when you find great mentors and advisers, keep them close for decades.

As you gain more experience, if you ever think the asset or class you are in can't get any higher, it is likely to be a good time to sell. Conversely, if you think the asset or class can't go down any more, it is likely to be a good time to buy. You might not be exactly right, but you may not be far off. Many mentors and fellow investors have recounted stories where they felt their market was overpriced, so they sold out. Andreas Panayiotou did that before the recession of 2007 and cashed in for hundreds of millions. The Ainscough family sold their crane hire company on more than one occasion at times around the peak of the market. This is another reason for staying in your business models and asset classes for the long term, because your ability to 'predict' these peaks and troughs will become increasingly more accurate.

22

The success (and profit) strategies I live by

We have covered what I believe really works specifically in business, finance and investing, so this chapter offers a more generic, evergreen view of how to profit by going against the tide.

Let your results speak for themselves

Success leaves clues. Let others speak of your successes but don't go blowing your own horn too hard. Balance self-promotion with humility. Your listeners will think that you are obviously biased when describing what you have achieved – as, of course, am I – causing them to occasionally discount some of what you say. It is much better to keep on keeping on, doing what you do well, and continuing to learn, analyse and iterate. People will notice on their own what you are achieving, and the most powerful testament to this success will be when they tell others. Be great, rather than telling everyone you are great. Work hard, and work smart. Endeavour to become better, and compound your success by developing your niched skills and experience longer and better than anyone else.

Model the best

Modelling the best is a great habit. If you can find the best person or company in any industry or sector and work out how they do something or what makes them successful, you have a short cut to a faster result. You have a person or system that has blazed the trail already, made the mistakes and mined the gold; if you are smart and forge a trusting relationship, you can get access to most of it. As the best in any sector usually earns many multiples more than the average, it is a great strategy. It is also inspiring and positively reinforcing to be around great people. It gives you a spring in your step and a pick-me-up that you can transfer right into your business or life. It does not matter whether it is a paid mentor, a friend of a friend, someone who takes you under their wing, or someone you can help in some way in exchange. There is always a market for the best; people still want it in a recession, really want it in the good times, and it never goes out of fashion. Selling to people who can afford the best can also be a lot more profitable.

Think long, long, long term

I like long-term thinking, planning and investing. Having an outlook of 20 years or more will reap huge benefits. All the hard work for less of the results and money is loaded up front, and most of the money and results and virtually none of the work are rear-loaded. This means you have to get there to maximize income. Stay persistent and consistent. Remember that change and starting over again have significant cost. The longer you go on with the same plan, the more your assets will grow. Compounding and momentum work best when given the longest amount of time, and reset to zero each time you start again.

Have multiple streams of income

A single stream of income is a risk. With one change completely out of your control, your income could immediately disappear. Of course, we all love the idea of multiple streams of passive income for wealth and lifestyle benefits. I also (mostly) love it for the protection of assets, for ease of living way below your means (income), and protection through all parts of the cycle. When some streams of income are strong, others will tick over on idle, and those may reverse as the markets change. Multiple streams of income also build capital fast, and capital protects and preserves wealth, as well as being collateral to grow income. Be careful, however, not to juggle too many streams or start too many too soon without maturing and systemizing existing streams.

Network and build relationships

This is a lifelong asset that perhaps I did not value as much as tangible assets in my early business years. I now highly value great people, both in business and in friendships. With great people, you have help, support, inspiration and contacts for all business, finance and investing eventualities: people to share and celebrate with; and leverage and growth. The benefits are far-reaching. Build your network as you would build a portfolio or a development: with care, attention, and as if you will rely on it for decades to come.

Work on yourself

You have to live with yourself for a very long time, so it makes sense to work on developing your own knowledge, your skills and your relationship with yourself, and to be able to predict how you will feel and react to situations you may be put in. If you feed your mind with valuable educational material via all media (books, audiobooks, podcasts, YouTube videos, courses, mentorships), then both you and your income will grow. I am amazed at how few people seek to continue with their learning once they leave school. This is why it helps to be in a business that is also your passion: in this case, education does not feel like work or as it did back at school.

Only when you truly know yourself can you set up your lifestyle to get the best outcomes in business, finance and investing. Examples of this are knowing how much sleep you need to perform at your maximum, knowing at what time of day you are most energized or in an energy coma, or when you feel inspired or have decision fatigue, knowing how much sun you need in the winter, or how you need to set up your workspace, and so on (read *Life Leverage* by Rob Moore for more in this area).

We are all a work in progress, we all have room to improve, and this self-improvement is what will enable us to generate more income and a more solid business. I will discuss the three stages of your personal development in Chapter 27.

23

How to set up, grow and scale your business

I am asked how to do this frequently. I have considered this topic at length in this chapter because to a certain extent it is a question similar to 'How long is a piece of string?' It depends on business models, individuals, markets, access to capital and other resources, and more. I am not one to shy away from a smart question, however, and as someone with a passion for business and who is writing a book about it, I have invested a great deal of time in creating as much of a 'system' for starting, growing and scaling a business as I thought one could without it becoming too generic.

Your budget

I believe that most businesses should be set up on a shoestring budget (or 'bootstrapped' as it is commonly called), using minimal capital and grown organically from reinvestment of profit. You might think that, to start out in the business world, you need to either obtain significant start-up capital or a big investor who will be your saviour, making the future of your business assured. This is often self-talk, and provides an excuse to justify why someone has not started a business. It helps to justify why they are where they are, and why they are not where they want to be.

Many will see a slot on *Dragons' Den* or the stories of billions in Silicon Valley as the answer to their prayers, as if a capital injection will make or allow them to start their business or turn it into the next Facebook or Uber. The reality is that the biggest benefit from being involved with one of the Dragons or a venture capitalist is most likely to be being able to utilize their experience, contacts and guidance rather than any capital they can provide. It is wiser in my opinion to gain experience while running your business without risking huge sums of capital you have not yet learned how to properly manage and deploy. People rarely see the downsides of outside capital injection because they are blinded by the money and desperate for a short cut, but that money comes at a huge cost: diminished control, reduction of equity, a crowd of decision-makers (and we all know that less is achieved when decisions are made by a committee), and often wastage.

'Bootstrapping' a business is usually the best way to test and prove a concept, show that there is a market for the product, and demonstrate that the business has been developed using sound principles. Bank financing (if available) can make entrepreneurs more liberal with spending; after all, many people spend other people's money more frivolously than their own, as happened with the spraying around of remortgaged property equity during the early- to mid-2000s boom years. Big capital injections can reduce urgency and move the focus away from generating income and keeping a cap on costs. It can also encourage unnecessarily big salaries and expenses, and make fledgling businesses less likely to succeed.

Clearly, with a proven (and I mean really proven over a number of years in another business or setting) business model and experienced management, external capital can be hugely beneficial. I am not attacking the industry in its entirety – only the illusory dream of most start-up entrepreneurs, as popularized by the media. Venture capital, private equity and other forms of finance can significantly accelerate growth, help buy market share, aid stock and premises purchases, increase marketing spend, and help with a hiring surge.

Your business model

Many successful businesses are started using inspiration from other successful businesses in the marketplace. At odds with the popular belief that it is best to dream up something new or original (perhaps school taught us that), as far as starting a new business is concerned I believe that is usually not a good idea, and can even be reckless. As already discussed, iterative innovation and hybridization are less risky and proven to give better results.

A solid business model built on solid, long-lasting fundamentals usually needs testing across a wide range of consumers and across a range of economic backdrops over a long period of time to become proven. The best way to do this is to use existing well-run businesses operating in a sector you are interested in and model their successful attributes. Mimicking or copying is not a good policy, and you are likely only going to be the best version of them and never better than the best; but you may notice a close resemblance between many leading businesses, which is more than a coincidence. In practice, a great way to model a successful business is to dissect a case-study business, work out how they work operationally, their culture, where their customers come from, and how they create and deliver their product or service. You can then make sure you insert your own flavour or slant into the product, operations, culture, and your own marketing, which you use to attract customers and show your uniqueness.

Before we incorporated our first company in December 2006, my business partner and I had to come up with a name for our first business. He was keen to create something new and I was keen to model something I thought already worked. I felt that modelling was a way to reduce risk. We looked at what looked like the best companies to model from the outside, and ended up creating a name very similar to a competitor's name. Almost immediately after incorporating, I regretted giving it a name that was so close to the competitor's, so we went back to the drawing board. After three months we changed the name to 'Progressive Property', which was a disruptive, innovative name when compared to our competitor's, and worked much better. A few short years later the company we modelled went bust, so our change was probably a smart move.

Your people

A most important factor in running a successful business is the people. While systems and automation are important for scale, you still need people to run them; machines simply do not create culture, brand, trust and loyalty. The key to building your team is to identify people who are great at the things you are not and to get them into your business. Having a business partner as one of these people – a person who has similar goals, values and a long-term vision but who is operationally opposite to you – can make a leveraged difference to your enterprise. I have noticed over the years that this works best with a business partner who is not at all like you in terms of what they are good at or enjoy doing in the business (usually what they enjoy and what they are good at are similar).

Mistakes in choosing a business or JV partner and in building a team can be quite costly. Many people want to go into business with people like them – people they like – because it feels good and is exciting in the short term. They romantically look for their 'soul-mate' in business, ironically usually decided after about three-and-a-half minutes, only later to fall out wildly because of a personality clash or the duplication of roles and tasks.

Others with a little more knowledge will go out and find a business partner based on the results of a personality or values test which they have both taken. They will often then try to form a partnership with someone who is on the opposite side of this spectrum. While this can be better than going into business by themselves, they mistakenly believe that, because they are different, it will work; they do not realize or take the time to work out their goals and objectives. Such simplistic matching of partners ignores many of the subtle facets of relationships which enable them to work (or not) in the long term and when challenges are encountered. Virtually all partnerships will work through the good times when the money is rolling in, but many do not stand the test of time, challenges and hardship.

Yes, it is good to understand what the other person is looking for from business and life, and to have a shortlist of people who you think would be compatible; but the important, often missing, step is to then have a period of courting in a business to see how you interact, and how you provide value to each other, before you jump in with both feet. This could mean starting a business and testing sales or the product before investing major capital or time resources. I see many people either with no partner or team, so they have to do everything themselves (including all the things they hate and are terrible at), or people jumping in like a blind date into partnerships and ventures with no thought for vision, alignment, strengths, weaknesses and some proof of compatibility.

Rob Moore and I first got to work together as employees in another business to see how we interacted and got on for around six months. A little like the courting period before a couple gets married, this period is essential because people will usually do in the future what they have done in the past. You need an incubation period to observe their behaviours once the sheen of trying to impress you has worn off and they feel more comfortable being around you, by which time their real strengths and weaknesses will show more clearly.

Your product and systems

The early stage of any new business is about testing and refining the product, processes and marketing systems. With time, you develop and improve these facets, making them sturdier; that bullet-proofs the business, makes the customer experience better, and should set the business in good financial standing. Once these systems are established, you would usually move each job on to other members of the team within an organizational hierarchy that you have created. Yes, modern companies have become more 'flat' and less structured, but I believe you need levels and layers of management to manage and scale a business. You can then grow revenue without swapping your time for money.

Once you maximize the working hours you can physically do yourself, the only way to grow is through improved systems and scaling of personnel. If you let yourself get to capacity, it will cause stress and mistakes, and the enjoyment and reasons you started your business will seem a distant memory. This is the pain point that all businesses go through: it is normal, and you are not alone. However, most self-employed people, under the illusion that they have a real business, do not scale through this.

In order to control and manage the business properly once it has passed the testing phase, checks and indicators need to be put in place to monitor the financial health of the business. A panel of key performance indicators (KPIs) is the most common and perhaps the best way to measure your business's performance. It is a simple set of performance metrics to which you can quickly refer and use as a way to measure progress. These need to be broken down into specific measures such as how many of X products have been sold that month across each business, what the income has been for a specific marketing activity, and how much cash has been received in the bank.

Setting up your business

Of course, starting growing, and scaling a business have many variables and future challenges that you cannot predict or put into a checklist system. However, if you follow these steps, implement these strategies, and leverage these platforms, indicators and resources, your business should be solid, scalable and sustainable.

There are KPIs to be measured in the following step-by-step business set-up and scale model:

Step 1: Discover your vision and values

First of all (for this part, forget monetization or the reasons why you cannot do this), ask yourself two questions:

- 'What is most important to me in life?'
- 'What is my purpose?'

Here are some more questions to help you answer these questions:

1 What could you do all day that doesn't 'feel' like work (most of the time)?
2 In what areas are you prepared to endure challenges and see them as a get-up-and-go rather than a give-up-and-go?
3 What do you feel totally in the flow doing, where you feel that time flies?
4 In what areas do you love helping people and solving problems?
5 What do you feel you are good at, better at than others, or could become great at?
6 What do you already spend a lot of your time doing and thinking about?
7 What causes bigger than yourself could you see yourself being involved in, or what mission/education do you want to share?

Step 2: Start a business around what comes up consistently

Here is how to monetize your latent talent and uniqueness:

1 Test the meaningful problem/solution.
2 Test whether your business will serve, solve and scale.
3 Crowdsource your product/service and create a minimum viable product (MVP) as soon as possible.
4 Test your product/service/intellectual property (IP) with low overhead and low risk, first and fast.
5 Get feedback and iterate.
6 Pivot frequently, and do not be too attached to what you want: Kodak, Rolls-Royce and Coca-Cola all started with other business models and evolved into their current forms.
7 Can you monetize it? Really? Do not be nostalgic or romantic. De-risk early.
8 Find out who your ideal customer is, and whether or not there are enough of them.
9 Repeat this process for each product/service you launch, and check yearly that your existing business is still doing this.

Step 3: Create your product or service and go live

1 Start with/create an MVP and iterate from there.
2 Do you have IP, a licence, a patent, a trade mark, or none of the above?
3 Set up your company quickly and easily online.
4 Decide whether you will be alone, with a business partner, or hiring a staff at the start (PA, MD/Ops or Sales).
5 Work our your costs and margins in isolation and including overhead; work out gross profit (GP) and net profit (NP).
6 Calculate your break-even point, maximum acquisition cost (MAC) per customer, per head revenue (PHR) and lifetime client value (LCV).
7 Finance through cash flow, personal cash/loans or equity.
8 Focus on making money, not on spending it. Decide on your own remuneration.

Step 4: Know your values, vision, mission and culture (VVMC)

1 What do you believe in and stand for?
2 What makes you unique?
3 How will you change the world/make a dent/matter?
4 How do you serve and solve?
5 How will you team/staff crowdsource your VVMC?
6 What makes your company the best company to work for?

Step 5: Create the community, database, fans, followers and customers

1 Use multi-platform strategies.
2 Leverage all the free ones first (YouTube, Facebook, LinkedIn, Twitter, etc.).
3 Be visible and credible on all main engines/sites.
4 Give information freely to build goodwill.
5 Make it easy to follow, like, opt-in, and to get information about your company.
6 Invest in pay per click (PPC) as soon as you can.
7 Discover as many marketing channels as possible: direct response (DR), not 'brand' marketing.

Step 6: Build your personal and business brand

1 Increase the value of your brand both within and exclusive of your company.
2 Set up platforms on both you and your company (Facebook, Twitter, Instagram, LinkedIn, YouTube, etc.).
3 Do not make the company reliant on you or it will not be possible to scale.
4 Give valuable information out for free and look after your community.

5 Be clear on your vision and values; define what you are and what you are not.
6 Balance new innovations with existing proven platforms.
7 Embrace digital early and focus on building a marketing team fast.

Step 7: Manage the main functions of the business

These functions are as follows:

- Marketing
- Vision and innovation
- Sales
- Accounting
- Finance
- HR and recruitment
- Administration
- Leadership/speaking.

Step 8: Manage yourself and build your team

1 Create a routine that works for you and follow it: cover key result areas (KRAs); income-generating tasks (IGTs); and key performance indicators (KPIs).
2 Compartmentalize your time. (Let your diary manage you; never manage yourself.)
3 Work on the vision and building the team. Leverage early in the day.
4 Manage and master your emotions (discipline, leadership).
5 Use your non-monetary (NM) assets when you do not have cash.
6 Help people; add value; look to do joint ventures (JVs).
7 Do not wait to leverage until you are maxed.
8 Merge passion/profession and vocation/vacation.
9 Tell everybody what you do; plug shamelessly, with passion.

Step 9: Grow the business

1 Expect challenges. Do not wish them away. Solve them and use them to grow.
2 If you keep asking your customers, business is easy; give them what they want and need.
3 Think long term. Will this decision be the right decision three, five, or ten years in the future? You have to live with past mistakes. Stay patient and keep going, even if progress seems slow.
4 Contribute to your community and industry.
5 Focus on serving and solving.
6 Keep overhead low and don't rush to raise external finance.
7 The longer you do it, the easier it gets.
8 Get mentors, take courses and keep reading/listening/learning. Do not do it on your own; you don't know what you don't know.
9 Do not listen to or get sucked into arguing with the critics, haters and trolls. Just do your thing as best you can and serve others.
10 Always seek feedback to grow and improve.
11 Do not procrastinate or deny real, big problems. Roll up your sleeves and sort them out, as that increases your value.
12 Know when to say yes and when to say no.
13 Get accurate and up-to-date management accounts and KPIs as soon as you can.

Raising funds for investment

When choosing which assets to invest in, it is a good idea to pick ones that banks understand and can secure their money against. Most income-producing properties meet this criteria but as soon as it becomes non-mainstream, such as a leasehold house or equities based on a lesser-known exchange like AIM, there will be much less interest from banks wanting to lend. Careful leverage can also be applied to funds that hold equity and bond-based investments. Barclays Wealth offers such a facility, lending around 60 per cent against a portfolio they manage.

Some more recent innovations, such as peer-to-peer lending and online crowd funding, have grown significantly. These solutions bypass banks and bring borrowers and savers together. I have met many who have used these methods to secure funds on trickier assets at low rates. It is, however, very much based on what the crowd is interested in lending for and what has done well in recent years on these platforms. The better-run platforms have stronger due diligence systems and methods of verifying the quality of the borrowers. I suspect it is these that will fare better in the long run as some of the smaller, more laissez-faire platforms are likely to suffer weighty impairments.

Monthly business management

Many business owners I know work out how much money they are making by comparing their bank account balance to their balance the previous month. That is clearly not the best – or even a particularly accurate – method of calculating the health of your business.

Although talked about a lot, but often not executed properly, monthly management accounts are critical to measuring the success of a business. It is important that these accounts display in detail what income has been received and what costs have been incurred for that month. The quality and validity of these line items will grow with time as you work with your accounts team to amend and make them more relevant.

During times of economic downturn or recession, it is especially important to keep a watchful eye on how revenue declines, so that costs can be reduced quickly to avoid a cash-flow crisis, which in the end is usually the sole reason a business goes bust. Accurate and well-presented reporting helps you, as the management of the business makes the decisions that will allow the business to grow based on the numbers.

The currency of this information is also key. Management accounts should be produced within two weeks of the end of the month. Accounts produced later will lose their value, as it is difficult to make decisions in terms of the direction of a business based on outdated numbers. It can be difficult to obtain these accounts in a timely fashion, with resources often cited as a reason why it is not possible. While this may be the case, it is important to ensure that your team has the resources to be able to provide these numbers, and to hold them accountable if they do not.

> If you want to continue the debate, or ask me any more detailed questions on this, then you can join a joint community that my business partner and I run online, where we have many thousands of entrepreneurs like you looking to get ahead, be part of a mastermind network, and pool knowledge and experience. It is free and hosted in a private community on Facebook; I suggest you request to join now, and I will see you there: https://www.facebook.com/groups/DisruptiveEntrepreneurs Community/

24

Hybridizing and super-specialization

Hybridizing and super-specialization (or iterative innovation) are two great ways to de-risk early innovation, using the uncommon sense philosophy to profit by going against the tide.

Before we go into these, it is important to understand the previous stage: niching, or specializing. You cannot be all things to all people; you cannot sell all products and all services – not even Amazon or Walmart can – and you cannot invest in every asset class with skill and sustainability. So you need to select niches and specialities about which you have passion, enthusiasm and knowledge, in order to maximize your time and your return. As you gain more experience and results, you can 'branch out' and widen your niche – just as Amazon started from selling just books until they proved the concept, scaled, made a profit and then took that experience, philosophy, marketing and VC money to de-niche.

But the broad approach is not a smart way to start. The narrower and deeper your niche, the more quickly you can master it and the faster you can dominate it, but the smaller it is. So start narrow enough to enable you to control it relatively quickly – but not too narrow, as in the example of someone writing a book on how to make the cream used to sandwich a macaron (a real example).

Hybridizing is a way to innovate and grow to create new niches, solutions and strategies without having to take the risks of being the first or testing them yourself. You simply merge existing models or strategies, or you borrow strategies from different niches and models and merge them into the class you are in. There can be rich pickings here because you get the early-mover advantage of being the first in a super-niche without all the risk attached to being the first in a larger niche. I see this as a trend that is going deeper and going to continue.

As markets have evolved over time, they have become more and more hyper-specialized. Less than 100 years ago, you could only get one model Ford, the Model T, and only in black. Now you can get many hybrid cars, like the Mercedes CLA or GLA, in any bespoke colour you choose, with nearly limitless options and extras. In music, you had the Beatles; now you have all manner of super-specialized hybrid bands like Babymetal and Metallica played only on string instruments and white kids merging rap and R&B and pop. You can now get salt in chocolate and marmite on nuts.

In property, not much more than a decade or two ago, single lets were the predominant residential property investment strategy. Then as innovators, disruptors and entrepreneurs looked for solutions and to pivot and weave around regulatory, finance and market changes, new sub-strategies emerged. Crowdfunding is an example of this, as traditional bank finance became harder to borrow after the recession of 2007/08. If you go back further, what was once a bank loan from a real person in a bank – someone for whom you dressed up in a suit and hoped to make a family friend – is now peer-to-peer and bridging and crowdfunding and part development finance, part some other finance, Funding Circle and angel investors: the hybrids/niches go on and on. And so it will continue, I believe, until someone has had enough and reverse-innovates – like companies now just making 'phones that phone'.

The way to grow and sustain innovative evolution as an uncommon sense businessperson/investor is to look at what super-specializations are happening in the wider market, what problems could be solved with a slight tweak, and how you can take two models and hybridize them, like a standard car with a 4 x 4. If you embrace this, then timing of the market becomes less relevant, and you can have success through all parts of the cycle with iterative innovation. I particularly like these two approaches because you have less risk and more control, without the high-and-low, feast-or-famine extremes that business can sometimes present.

Many people assume that a successful business is developed out of an amazing idea or invention they dream up in the shower, and then they make millions. I have seen only a handful of examples where this is the case, and yet the story still gets glorified. What most fail to realize is that success comes from the application and steadfast execution of good (not amazing) ideas, of which there are many.

Part 4: Additional resources

This section includes answers to some frequently asked questions from investors and business owners. For example, I am often asked what publications I read and respect, and how to go about continuing with self-development. The resources here do not neatly fit into any previous section, but they still offer important ways to help you profit by going against the tide. If you have any further questions for me personally or feel strongly that another question should be included, I am open to feedback and would like to continue the discussion. Simply post your question here and tag my full name:

https://www.facebook.com/groups/DisruptiveEntrepreneurs
Community/

25

Publications and resources I respect and those I reject

My favourite source of new information is usually a respected and experienced business friend, mentor, course, book or other publication or training material specific to the subject I am researching. The rest of my learning comes from taking that new information and implementing it. Experience and actually doing the thing is the missing piece to the puzzle and the litmus test of success, so you have to balance theory with action, repetition, testing, tweaking and measuring. I like to repeat the exercise over and over, making it part of who I am, because the best and easiest results are from habits that are subconscious. We are all a little different: some of us benefit from more support, some of us prefer theory and some prefer just to get on with doing it. All these methods can work, but all can be dangerous if used recklessly or complacently. I think it's really important that we all know who we are in this regard, as it will have a big impact on our progress and on where we need support and accountability.

Useful property resources

The Land Registry

The Land Registry can be very useful for finding property. It is usually clear from the title register who owns the property, what they paid for it, and who lent on it. You may decide that contacting the current owner (who might not live at the property) could be a good route towards negotiating a more creative deal, such as an exchange with delayed completion or an option deal. You may be looking to develop the property, in which case you will probably look at any covenants on the title to make sure there are no restrictions that apply to what you want to do.

Lenders and other debt-related issues can also show up on the title. The title plan is particularly interesting, as you can see what land is included, and work out whether there is enough room for an extension or perhaps another property. Another property may require access, which usually means that there needs to be enough room to build a road to access the proposed site from somewhere else.

The Nationwide House Price Index and Rightmove

These can be very useful. They show the change in house prices for a given period and indicate the general direction of price moves. While authoritative, these two indexes lag by a few months, as they do not register transactions for around three months after a buyer makes a purchase. The Rightmove index is forward-looking, making it a less concrete measure of the market which tracks asking prices rather than actual sold-for prices. As Rightmove is at the front of the buying process, it indicates the change in sentiment earlier, as it is these asking prices that are then connected (usually higher) to the actual sold-for values, which are tracked by Nationwide and the Land Registry.

Google Maps and Street View

Google Maps satellite view is a tool I find invaluable in the research process. Often even more insightful than the title plan, it shows what the site physically looks like, giving a good idea of access and extra buildable area. It is also possible to work out the size of a plot using a Google Maps area calculator.

Street View can also be a brilliant way to look at the front of a property, if it can be accessed from a road. You can often also see the type and quality of the street scene, which will help you understand what is likely to be most profitable to develop. Understanding the height of the eaves of surrounding buildings can help you work out how high you are likely to be able to go, and understand what height the planning department is likely to grant you permission for.

The Energy Performance Certificate (EPC) Register

The EPC Register is particularly interesting in that it usually has the floor area of the property in square metres listed on it. While the EPC and estate agents' sizes shown in sales details are not always accurate, they offer another means by which to objectively value a property. Square metres multiplied by 10.76 become square feet, and it becomes easier to compare the property you are looking at with other finished properties on a square-foot basis. This method of valuation can be useful when it is applied to three similar properties in a given locality, providing an accurate valuation.

Local council websites

The planning section of local council websites can be very interesting. It shows what others are up to in the local area. I like to try and work out what another developer has applied for and gained consent or refusal for in the planning process. That provides good insight into what you may be able to do. I especially like to do this when I have done the research and bid on a property through an agent or at an auction, but have missed out on it. It is also interesting to see which architect or consultant they used, as this person is likely to be able to do the same for you in similar schemes in the future.

Useful publications

The Financial Times

This publication is daily and current, and has a good variety of writers with experience and understanding of the economic landscape. It is largely bipartisan. It is less sensationalist than other broadsheets, and far more factual. They are more likely to do their own research and analysis rather than taking second-hand sources. Their suggestions and observations are more likely to come true and are City-focused, reciting the rumour on the street. Closer to more of the real action, their writers seem more interested in working out the economic ramifications of a change or political decision.

The Economist

This is a weekly magazine, which means it is not as perpetually current as the *FT*, but the analysis goes even deeper and uses more empirical data. It gives a more international perspective and is more scholarly, with real economic theories applied relative to detailed historical data. For example, *The Economist* developed the Big Mac Index as a light-hearted guide (they say light-hearted, but I think it's not) to work out whether currencies are at their correct level based on the principal or purchasing power parity.

Websites

The BBC News website is useful for up-to-date and current breaking news on business and finance.

Inc is a website that comments on business, entrepreneurship, and 'life hacks' for business owners. The authors of its articles know what they are talking about and have direct and relevant experience. I read many of the articles and get holistic – though conceptual – benefits.

Business Insider, as with Inc above, helps you become aware of business 'thought leaders' you didn't know of before, who you can then follow and read up on.

Estates Gazette online is a property publication that gives you industry-related news and insight into market and regulatory changes. It also publicizes commercial properties for sale.

The 'Disruptive Entrepreneur' podcast

While I have to listen to my business partner, Rob Moore, all day every day, and sometimes the last thing I want to do is have him in my ears in my relaxation time, I secretly listen to this, with particular interest in his interviews with entrepreneurs.

General articles

I spend a lot of my pleasure-research time being directed away from the above sites and articles to find other more specific articles online. I also find that some Facebook groups relevant to business, finance and investing can be useful, but you do have to filter through some 'noise'.

Other resources

Companies House

Companies House is an excellent source of information on companies in the UK. Recently revamped to make it more user-friendly, the website gives insight into many companies which you may be looking to for investment, to do business with or to compete against. While smaller companies file abbreviated accounts, and therefore full diligence cannot be gained, the larger ones are usually forced to file more detailed information, which is publicly available. When deciding whether to provide a loan to a company, one may decide to check what the company's balance sheet or profitability looks like before making the loan. Insights into what loans and charges a company has already taken or provided can also be disseminated, making your decision more informed.

CEBR

The Centre for Economic and Business Research provides good proprietary information on changing economic winds, and more specifically house price data. Rather than regurgitating other sources of information, they create their own content.

Bank of England Inflation Report

This quarterly report is one of the most authoritative sources of information and comes directly from the top policy and decision-makers in the UK. These reports can be downloaded in presentation and video format from the Bank of England website directly, and are a great way to cut through much of the noise. The Bank of England has insights into the economy that other market participants simply do not have access to. Its tentacles stretch deep into areas of the economy, providing valuable datasets. These datasets are then analysed and evaluated by some of the best minds in the country to determine the best course of action.

Clearly their predictions cannot be precisely correct, as there are many unknown factors in the domestic and world economy that can affect them. This can be especially true when economic shocks come along, such as the dotcom crash, 9/11, the credit crunch, Brexit and other such events or catastrophes. Present in most of the pictorials from the Bank of England are coloured shaded areas which depict the probability of a given inflation rate, growth rate and other economic indicators. These are known as fan charts. Looking at data like this can help with making decisions on the future path of interest rates in relation to bank lending and property investment.

Economic indicators

I monitor and use these economic indicators to make decisions in business and property:

Gross domestic product (GDP) is the most common measure of economic activity. It is a measure of transactions and captures the aggregate value of purchases of goods and services within an economy. A change in this metric shows whether there has been growth or recession in an economy. The best place to get forecasts of future economic growth is from the Bank of England Inflation Reports; they are probably the best informed, and often turn out to be the most accurate.

Consumer price inflation is the central measure of inflation or deflation over time. Again, the Bank of England Inflation Reports are the best predictor of where inflation is likely to head in the mid-term.

The FTSE 100 is a good measure of economic sentiment. As the economic markets perceive that economic activity is set to increase and blue-chip company profits are therefore due to increase, the FTSE 100 index will usually rise. It usually looks around one year ahead, so it can be a good indicator of how the market collectively sees economic activity in a year. The FTSE 100 is a great predictor of growth and market conditions at a given point in the future.

Publications and resources to avoid

The majority of the population gets its information from the people around them. I cannot overstate the negative impact of surrounding yourself with the wrong people. Clearly, not everyone around you is going to be conversant with business and investing, but it is true that you will become more like those you are friends with. If you surround yourself with people who get their information from the *Daily Mail* and for whom investing is something to do when you visit the lottery counter at the corner shop, you will probably not get the best stimulus. We all need fertile ground from which we can learn and grow, so if many your friends are successful businesspeople, you are more likely to become a successful businessperson, and their traits, habits and experience will rub off on you.

So avoid these publications and resources:

Pub talk

Any pub talk or advice from those with no experience should be ignored. As already stated, and is important to restate: free advice is worth every penny.

Virtually all tabloid newspapers

They are, of course, good for entertainment purposes, such as the sensationalist five minutes of non-value that may make you chuckle but bear no resemblance to the facts. Because the *Daily Mail* online is the most visited news website in the UK at the time of writing, it is by nature non-contrarian, mainstream mass media. I just searched the *Daily Mail* online today, and here is the headline: 'Er, awkward! Ryan Giggs sits on a sun lounger on the opposite side of the pool to his estranged wife Stacey during family holiday'. Enough said. Do not get lured in.

Some broadsheet newspapers

This can be dangerous because the broadsheets look credible, but many of their journalists have no direct knowledge of what they are writing about, many of the sources have a vested interest, and many articles are partway towards being an advertorial. They rarely come up with proprietary information, and often regurgitate information from other publications and common perceived wisdom, not uncommon sense. The main exception is the *FT*.

If a publication becomes too mainstream, it goes against the uncommon sense philosophy. Because it is exposed to the masses, it is likely to be biased and sensationalist, and any tips priced into an asset or innovations may already be too popularized to be innovative. Be wary of any share tipsters and buy, hold or sell recommendations in mainstream publications.

26

Which type of investor/entrepreneur are you?

Not everyone wants the same outcome from business and investing. I have tended to judge people by my own standards, and previously assumed that everyone wanted to build a huge empire. Since we have built and scaled training businesses, I have refined my knowledge: I now realize that some people want more 'lifestyle' businesses, others want a part-time business, and still others want to feel like an entrepreneur but with the safety of a regular paycheque. Whichever one of these seems most like you, you can still use the uncommon sense philosophy and you can still profit by going against the tide in business, finance and investing. It would be good for your overall lifestyle, wellbeing and path of least resistance to profit to consider which route you might prefer to take, and whether you want to use one as a stepping stone to get to others in the future.

Lack of clarity and self-awareness regarding what you want and what type of entrepreneur you are can often explain why you might feel frustrated or overwhelmed, and lead to feelings of self-doubt or pointlessness, comparing yourself to others, thinking that your progress is too slow, procrastinating and other resistance.

Here are the three types of investor/entrepreneurs and the differences between them.

The empire builder

Empire builders do exactly that: they build empires. They want to go big: big businesses, big portfolios. They take big risks, too, and like to negotiate and be creative while making deals happen. Empire builders are usually competitive, keep score of their wealth and their assets, are happy to aggressively leverage, joint-venture and borrow money. They are often disruptive and can create chaos. They are good starters, drivers and builders, and are continually driven by targets and growth. It's never big or fast enough for the empire builder, and their business – and often their life outside business – is a roller coaster with big risks that make them feel alive.

The lifestyle investor

Lifestyle investors/entrepreneurs crave freedom and choice the most, and do not want to be tied down by huge overheads. They work to live instead of living to work, desire their income to be passive, and may accept a smaller asset base and net worth in exchange for autonomy. They (need to) embrace automation and systemization more than vast scale. Not always striving and never arriving, they want order and control, not chaos. The want to 'set and forget' and an easier life to do more of what they love, where they love, when they love. They can be a little ideological and naive about the building blocks of a real, sustainable business or investment, and can be flighty. But they are good at getting out of the way of others in their business, and at leveraging and outsourcing.

The intrapreneur

'Intrapreneurs' want autonomy and creativity, freedom to make decisions and respect, but not the risk of starting their own enterprise. They like to lead but do not have to, they do not need praise as much as an empire builder, and they do not want the feast-or-famine lifestyle. They may have a lower risk threshold, they may have children and overheads they feel they cannot sacrifice for the short term, or they may have tried without success to build their own business. They also like to be around people and in a team, and usually do not want to start alone in their spare bedroom. They want freedom, but will accept some authority from others to be part of a team. Maybe they enjoy the job they have, so a part-time income and business would suit them better. They tend to be more patient than the other two types, but also have to accept a lower income or smaller success as a result.

> Which one are you? Do you match one type now but would like to become another type in the future? Perhaps you are even a hybrid of more than one, or at times one and at times another? I hope this chapter helps you to become more self-aware and to understand that there is more than one type of investor/entrepreneur. With this knowledge, you can build your lifestyle, empire or role accordingly, and be yourself, which is always the best choice.

Balancing risks

I started my career in a job in a corporate graduate scheme. I did this for the experience, and was happy enough to be an employee, but only for a short amount of time. I got a taste of what the higher-level executives had, but that did not interest me. They had not enough wealth or business acumen to have a vast business, were not happy in their role, and had limited career progression opportunities. I then took a role in a property company (before Progressive Property), where you might say I was more of an 'intrapreneur'. I was at the coalface of decisions much more, learned a great deal more, enjoyed more autonomy, but was ultimately still an employee. While I was not in a rush to take a risk, I felt that I would at some stage. In late 2005, my hand was forced (that story is explained in detail in my book *Low Cost High Life*), and I became a business owner. I love building empires, but am not as risk-hungry as many extreme empire builders I know, so perhaps I might be mostly an empire builder with something of the other two types as well.

Every year, an old friend – I'll call him Frank – and I would organize a foreign trip abroad. When we were 17, we travelled to Nepal to meet my parents, who were living there at the time. Noticing that local driving regulations seemed to be tamer than at home, my pal Frank, who had the uncommon sense mentality drummed into him by his father from a young age, noticed that extra tips went a lot further in that part of the world. One evening, after a dinner out, Frank said, 'Watch this!' as he hailed a taxi. After speaking to the driver in broken Nepali, he rummaged around in his pocket and handed over a wad of rupees. As if by magic, the driver got out, sat on the passenger side and Frank got in the driver's seat and shouted to me, 'Jump in, I'm driving!' and drove us home.

This went on for the rest of the week, until we graduated to pedal-powered rickshaws, which seemed more fun. With Frank at the controls, however, he had an issue tracking a straight line along the road one evening. As I shouted, 'Turn right now!' one of the wheels collapsed into a storm drain, locked, and catapulted the rickshaw owner and me on to the road. Needless to say, that little skirmish cost us a more than the usual few rupees as the chap had a buckled wheel, smashed light and ripped clothes to bill us for! Clearly we had come unstuck, pushing the uncommon sense philosophy too far. Going for a high-risk option, we had got a bit of early on-road driving time in, but put ourselves and others in danger. We learned a valuable lesson that we needed to focus on less risky applications of the principle thereafter.

27

The three stages of self-development in business

If there is one thing that supersedes and overrides all business, finance and investing decisions and results, it is you. The culture or your organization and therefore the results from it, from the ground up, are your responsibility and a reflection of who you are and how you operate (and behave). Your business will only grow at the speed at which you grow. Your investments will yield a return proportionate to your ability to research, analyse and manage your emotions when faced with decisions and fluctuations in the market.

Over the years, I have found one of the great benefits of growing a business and your net worth is that it literally forces you to grow yourself, either through mistakes or results. You earn or you learn, and that is what I love about being a business owner; you have full responsibility and control, but you have to grow. I have personally found the following areas to be exposed and stress tested, with your level of success incumbent on your ability to learn and master these:

1 A true understanding of your strengths and weaknesses
2 The ability to take criticism and meet challenges
3 Control of your emotions
4 A willingness to seek and accept feedback
5 The ability to let go and say no
6 The capacity to get out of your own way to hire and scale
7 Care of and focus on your staff and customers' needs above your own
8 Evolution through markets, innovations and disruptions
9 The ability to surround yourself with great people in a variety of areas
10 Management of your ego in both high and low self-worth areas.

Each one of these is covered in more detail below, in the three stages to mastery of business through the mastery of yourself:

1 Self-awareness

How aware are you of your strengths and weaknesses? Do you over- or underplay them? How aware are you of how others perceive you and how others see your strengths and weaknesses? Are you aware of your energy highs and lows and what tasks you are performing at these times? Are you aware of and can you articulate your values and what you accept and will not stand for? What do you love to do and what you want to leverage out? What mistakes do you make over and over?

This is a continual journey, but the more you know yourself the more you can grow your business. Keep asking yourself good questions. Learn from the times when you blindside yourself or when you get backed into a corner. Learn what the recurring themes are, such as saying yes to too many things, agreeing with something to get rid of someone rather than because it is the right decision, putting too much on your plate because you think you can handle it, taking on tasks you don't enjoy or have proven to mess up, and so on. Then put systems, processes and decisions in place that mean you never put yourself in that position.

For example, I know I need to run at least three times a week. I know I need to get at least eight hours of sleep every night. I know I need one to two hours during which I am completely undisturbed by anyone. I know I need a car that is a convertible. I know I hate shopping. I know I do not like to decide what clothes to wear. While these are perhaps not relevant to you, they are used as examples to help you find out exactly how you will react in a future situation and how to make a strategic decision beforehand to give you the best outcome.

2 Self-education

The more aware you become of your habits, behaviours, reactions and 'isms', the more you will know which areas you need to invest in or outsource completely. How much time and money are you investing in working on yourself? Are you outsourcing your weaknesses and getting out of the way of those better and more suited to those tasks than you? Are you surrounding yourself with the right team to balance your personality traits? Are you challenging yourself, or is your ego surrounding you with those who will only say yes? Do you have mentors who are at a higher level than you? Do you read and listen to audio daily? Do relevant training courses constantly fill your brain with the food it needs to grow your business?

I will admit to being historically mean with money. I would rather preserve capital than spend it or even invest it, and would struggle to see any benefits in much that's non-tangible. I love ownership and I love owning physical assets, which is perhaps why I love property so much. But to invest a few grand on a seminar or mentor seemed to me to be frivolous, with benefits that were hard to assess, and would feel completely alien. I worked through this by setting aside an amount (as a percentage) of capital that I would invest in non-tangible assets like courses, mentorships, my health and wellbeing, travel time, and so on, so that I could justify it to myself, and test and measure the benefits with capital I was prepared to risk.

It quickly became clear that one good piece of information could yield a great return – especially as your enterprise grows and so the information is scalable – and that one good mentor or person in your network could reduce mistakes considerably. As someone who likes to see a trail of proof before I jump into any investment, mentors and experts, as I perceive them, are especially important and beneficial to my personal (and therefore business) growth. This has taught me to look at not just the cost of a more intangible investment in my personal development education, but the opportunity cost of not doing it, much as I would capital and assets. This is a considerable change over the last decade that has benefited both me and my business.

3 Self-mastery

Once you know and invest in yourself, you can really know yourself. You can plan your day around your energy levels, or even educate your assistant to plan your day so that she/he can second-guess you. You challenge yourself regularly to grow and put yourself in safe but uncomfortable situations. You constantly and consistently work on yourself and *on* your business more than *in* it, and not only when things go wrong. You take feedback graciously and look to learn from everyone, despite how your ego feels about it. You even seek out feedback and people who will challenge you rather than agree with you. You leverage and delegate to your team, inspire them with a vision, and support them in growing their career too, serving others as much as yourself. You know the balance between high self-worth and low self-worth in different areas of your life. You are aware when your high self-worth serves you and when your ego or confidence runs away with you, but you are also humble enough to know and not pretend to be good at things you are not good at, and to talk yourself up when you are actually better than you think.

> While growth is never complete, if you go and grow through these stages, you will have a sustainable, consistently growing, and future-proofed business. It is important to mention personal development in a business, finance and investing book, because you are your business, and your business is you.

Afterword

When all is said and done, more is said than done, and to know and not to do is not to know. Thank you for reading or listening to this entire book on uncommon sense business, finance and investing. I hope you have found some takeaway actions that will help you grow your asset base, business and net worth. I have spent too many years waiting and worrying about getting into business and investing, for fear of the risks. While it hasn't always been easy, it has always been worth it, and my only regret is that I didn't take the plunge sooner. I pass the torch to you to take these strategies and tactics and leverage them for the long term, then pass them on to the next generation to do the same. Enjoy the journey and preserve your capital – for every pound is a prisoner.

Mark Homer